The Leeds Pottery

1, *Coffee-pot. Height* 9¼ *in. About* 1775.
Donald Towner. Page 36.

DONALD TOWNER

The Leeds Pottery

Cory, Adams & Mackay

First published 1963 by Cory, Adams & Mackay Ltd, 39 Sloane St, London, S.W.1
Printed and made in Great Britain by W. & J. Mackay & Co Ltd, Chatham

Contents

Preface   page ix

ONE   *History, Part I*   1

TWO   *History, Part II*   12

THREE   *Early Wares*   22
         DELFTWARE
         BLACK EARTHENWARE
         RED EARTHENWARE
         WHITE SALTGLAZED STONEWARE
         RED STONEWARE
         CREAM-COLOURED EARTHENWARE

FOUR   *Early Creamware*   26
         SLIP DECORATED CREAMWARE
         COLOUR-GLAZED CREAMWARE
         ENAMELLED CREAMWARE

FIVE   *Later Creamware*   33
         CREAMWARE FIGURES
         COLOUR-GLAZED CREAMWARE
         ENAMELLING
         TRANSFER-PRINTING
         GLAZES

SIX   *Late Wares*   41
         CREAMWARE
         PEARLWARE
         TRANSFER-PRINTING
         FIGURES
         WARES PAINTED IN MINERAL COLOURS
         BLACKWARE
         DIP DECORATED WARE
         YELLOW WARE
         LUSTRE

v

Seven *The Drawing Books* 49
 ORDER BOOKS

Eight *The Pattern Books* 56

Nine *The Marks* 142

Ten *Moulded Details* 147
 HANDLES
 SPOUTS
 FLOWER-KNOBS
 TERMINALS

Eleven *Other Local Potteries* 155
 POTTERIES OF THE DON
  Swinton Pottery
  Don Pottery
  Newhill Pottery
  Mexborough Pottery
  Kilnhurst Old Pottery
  Templehurst Pottery

 POTTERIES OF THE AIRE
  Rothwell Pottery
  Hunslet Hall or Petty's Pottery
  Taylor's Pottery or New Pottery
  Allison's Pottery
  Meadow Lane Pottery or Russell's Pottery
  Marsden's Pottery
  Leathley Lane Pottery
  Swillington Bridge Pottery
  Woodlesford Pottery
  Holbeck Moor Pottery
  Hunslet Moor Pottery
  Castleford Pottery
  Ferrybridge Pottery

 POTTERIES OF THE HUMBER
  Belle Vue Pottery, Hull

Appendix 161
 A. LETTERS
 B. EXTRACTS
 C. INDENTURES

Bibliography 175

Index 177

Illustrations

COLOUR PLATES

Coffee-pot   *frontispiece*

Teapot and cream jug   facing page 4

Taper-stick and teapot   22

Cup and saucer and teapot   38

LINE DRAWINGS

Figure 1   Map of district south of Leeds   page 6

2   Plan of the Leeds Pottery   13

3, 4 Specimen pages from Drawing Books   50, 52

5, 6 Marks   144, 145

7   Handles   148

8   Spouts   150

9   Flower-knobs   152

10   Terminals   153

THE PATTERN BOOK

Facsimile reproduction of 1814 edition   59

MONOCHROME PLATES

1–5a   Early wares

5b–19   Early creamware

20–38   Later creamware

39–48   Late wares

Preface

THE PURPOSE OF THIS BOOK *is to place on record all the available information on the Leeds Pottery and to discuss the various types of ware it produced particularly from the point of view of providing the collector and others with the means of identifying Leeds pottery from the mass of wares produced by earthenware factories throughout England during the second half of the eighteenth century. To this end particular emphasis has been laid on such features of the ware as forms, moulded details and glazes, as the author believes that in these lie the surest means of identifying unmarked pieces of earthenware. In this connexion, line drawings of Leeds handles, spouts, knobs and terminals are included (Figs. 7–10). While there are many factories known by name but whose wares have not yet been identified there must also remain others whose very name and locality have been lost. The task of identification is often a difficult one, particularly as such a very small proportion of eighteenth-century earthenware bears a factory mark, and the author has been at much pains, therefore, to establish groups of ware of similar characteristics and gradually from the acquisition of a marked piece belonging to first one group and then another, or by some other sure means of attribution, he has been able to establish what he believes to be the source of a number of these groups. In some cases the origins still remain unknown, but the wares ascribed in this book to the Leeds Pottery have only been so ascribed on positive evidence of one kind or another, and where any doubt exists the author has not hesitated to say so. The period covered extends from the Pottery's earliest known existence till its bankruptcy in 1820. This constitutes a period when, in artistic excellence, the wares of the Leeds Pottery were second to none.*

For the first time since its original publication the entire Leeds Pottery Pattern Book has been reproduced. The 1814 edition has been used which not only contains all the illustrations in the earlier editions but a number of additional engravings as well.

With regard to the plates both in colour and in monochrome, all the pieces illustrated are believed by the author to have been produced by the Leeds Pottery. The pieces selected for illustration have been chosen, neither for their rarity nor aesthetic qualities, but to show the full range of the wares produced by the Leeds Pottery and, as far as possible, no piece has been included which has been previously illustrated.

The sources of some of the past information about the Pottery have been discovered, and many new facts relating to the history of the Leeds Pottery have been established and are now published for the first time, as well as fresh information concerning its wares.

In all these researches I have been greatly helped by art galleries, museums, libraries and other bodies. I would particularly like to acknowledge my indebtedness to the Director and Keeper of the Leeds City Art Galleries for making arrangements for the photographing of pieces from the City's vast collection of pottery, and for permission to publish them in this book. I would also like to thank those in charge of the Ceramic Departments of The Victoria and Albert Museum and British Museum for their continued kindness and help in every way; also the Director of the City Museum, Leeds; the Keeper of the Yorkshire Museum, York; the Director of the Castle Museum, Norwich; the Director of the Fitzwilliam Museum, Cambridge; and the Registrar and staff of the West Riding Registry of Deeds at Wakefield for the great assistance I received from them. And lastly, I would like to express my gratitude to all those museums, collectors and others, whose names appear in this book, for their permission to illustrate specimens from their collections.

CHAPTER ONE

History, Part I

THE FIRST BOOK to mention the Leeds Pottery was *A History of Pottery and Porcelain* by Joseph Marryat published in 1850. On page 65 of this book Marryat says, 'An establishment at Leeds has been recently brought to notice by the discovery of a book of Patterns of which a copy may be seen at the British Museum published in 1770 by the proprietor of the Pottery, Mr Green, and which is interesting as identifying the ware by comparison with the engravings. It approaches in quality to the early dingy white Staffordshire or is of a creamy colour with much open work and is marked by the letter "C" or "G" or an arrowhead in a dirty brown colour.'[1]

Although the first edition of the Leeds Pattern Book was published in 1783, not 1770, this account was a beginning, and was followed in 1855 by the publication of the first edition of the catalogue of the Museum of Practical Geology, Jermyn Street, London, of which Sir Henry de la Bèche was the Director. Two pieces of Leeds creamware, a plate and a bedside lamp or food-warmer, had then been identified and are included in the catalogue, in which about three-quarters of a page of text is devoted to the Leeds Pottery, in which de la Bèche repeats Marryat's statements including the description of the marks, but describes the Leeds Pattern Book in greater detail and accuracy from a copy which had been acquired by the Museum.

Recently, in selecting a copy of the Leeds Pattern Book from among the several editions of it in the Victoria and Albert Museum Library for reproduction and inclusion in the present book, I discovered this identical copy bearing the stamp of the Museum of Practical Geology. Pasted inside the cover were three old letters which proved to be the source of much of the past information about the Leeds Pottery, written by a certain Thomas Wilson of Leeds in the year 1854 and directed to Sir Henry de la Bèche at the time when he was compiling his catalogue, and obviously in answer to inquiries from him for information about the Leeds Pottery.

---

[1] A painted arrowhead sometimes occurs under the so-called Batavian ware (Pl. 45b) made by the Leeds Pottery after about 1790.

The full text of letters will be found in the Appendix of this book (page 161), but the following are extracts from two of them:

Crimbles House, Leeds
20 March 1854

Sir,

I fear there will be more difficulty than I at first anticipated in getting information about the Leeds Pottery—and certainly more delay than I hoped—in consequence of the great distance of time since its first establishment and of its having passed by the misfortunes of the proprietors into new hands. All the original specimens of the ware, and most of any antiquity have been dispersed and all the books and papers that remain are in the hands of the official Assignee. The present proprietor to whom I have obtained an introduction professes to be disposed to give you every assistance in his power—but is at present very much engaged. He has promised however to get the old papers, and to collect all the information he can from old workmen as well as to try and get some specimens of the original ware.

I understand the Pottery was first established in 1760 by two brothers of the name of Green—that they first made a black ware and subsequently a cream coloured ware.

I am, Sir,
Yours faithfully

Sir H. J. De La Bèche.   THOMAS WILSON.

Crimbles House, Leeds
26 May 1854

My dear Sir,

I am sorry that I have not been able to send you answer to your inquiries about the Leeds Potteries earlier and that even now they are so meagre. I will however persue the inquiry this autumn, when I hope to be more at leisure, and if I meet with anything worth recording, I will not fail to let you know. The fact is the history of the Leeds Pottery is like that of many of our earlier Manufacturing establishments, it attained a certain degree of reputation and extent of trade at one period, which was not maintained at a later period and by the subsequent proprietors. In 1815 the estate passed into the hands of Assignees,[1] and all papers and books connected with its early career seem then to have been dispersed. This has been the cause of the great difficulty I have found in getting any accurate information. I am indebted for the principal part of what I now send you to Mr William Warburton, son of one of the present proprietors and if you name your authorities he is the party who should be mentioned.

I am Dear Sir
Yours truly

Sir H. T. De La Bèche.   THOMAS WILSON.

[1] In fact this took place in 1820, not 1815 (pages 20, 167).

Enclosed with this letter was the following questionnaire with answers supplied by William Warburton,

1 Date of first establishment

1 1760

2 Clays first employed whether from the vicinity or otherwise

2 Cornwall and Dorsetshire

3 Character of first manufactured ware

3 Fancy and Cream coloured

4 Names of those who founded or were early engaged in the manufacture

5 An account of the different changes in proprietors afterwards

4 & 5
Humble, Green & Co.
Hartley Greens & Co.
Samuel Wainwright
S. & S. Chappell
Warburton & Britton

6 When Poole Clays first introduced

6 1760

7 When Flints first employed

7

8 Any information connected with the supply or use of Poole clay or Flints

8 Ever since the pottery was established Poole clay must have been used

9 Information connected with changes in the manufacture and character of the ware

9 The ware was very inferior to that of the present time

10 Situation of the first Works also situation of other than the first Works

10 On the present site. Others in the immediate neighbourhood

11 Dates when any may have been discontinued

11 All are still working

12 If any present Works

12 Yes

13 Materials which may now be employed

13 Too numerous to mention

14 Any general information which may be thought calculated to contribute to the History of the Leeds Potteries

14

15 Marks for the Ware

15 Various at the present time

Evidently the letters arrived too late for this information to be included in the first edition of the 1855 catalogue, though the date 1760 was added to the heading, probably in the proof stage, and reads 'Leeds Pottery 1760'. Most of the information contained in the letters, however, was published in the second edition of 1871 and follows almost word for word the replies to the questionnaire. As a result, de la Bèche commences his account of the Leeds Pottery in the second edition of the catalogue with the words 'Pottery was first manufactured at Leeds in 1760, by two brothers named Green', and this information has been repeated by subsequent writers ever since.

The list of pieces of Leeds pottery in the collection had by this time risen from two to thirty-nine, and Leeds wares were being extensively sought and collected, particularly in Yorkshire. A number of the collections, formed at this time, containing many important and rare pieces of Leeds pottery, were left to the Leeds City Art Gallery, where they are now housed. The Boynton Collection, which was also formed about this time, was left to the Yorkshire Museum at York, where it formerly graced the entrance hall with Arthur Hurst's magnificent collection of Yorkshire wares.

Lady Charlotte Schreiber collected a number of pieces of Leeds ware on her expeditions in search of English pottery and porcelain, and it is interesting to note that in the original catalogue of the Schreiber Collection published in 1884 she ascribes the date 1758, not 1760, for the foundation of the Leeds Pottery. Her reason for so doing will appear later.

The first considerable scholarly contribution towards our present knowledge of the Leeds Pottery was made by Llewellyn Jewitt in *The Ceramic Art of Great Britain*, 1878. In this he says, 'Of the date of the establishment of the pot-works at Leeds, nothing definite is known. It is, however, certain that they were in existence about the middle of the last century and that they were then producing wares of no ordinary degree of excellence. . . . The first proprietors of whom there appears to be any record were two brothers named Green, in 1760.'

Jewitt adds a considerable amount of new information, not only concerning the wares produced at Leeds, but also about the Pottery itself. He seems to have ascertained the whereabouts of some of the accounts and papers of the original Pottery, though he does not say in whose possession they were, and by a personal inspection of them is able to give a number of interesting facts concerning the financial side of the Pottery.

This account was followed in 1892 by *The Leeds Old Pottery*, by Joseph and Frank Kidson. Until now, this has been the only book to deal exclusively with the subject of the Leeds Pottery, but today it is both scarce and expensive.

The two brothers Kidson lived at Leeds, where they formed a large collection of Leeds creamware. In later years, probably after the death of Frank, Joseph opened an antique shop and sold off the collection piece by piece, no doubt augmenting his stock from time to time.

Ever since its publication, Kidson's book has been sought and cherished by

2, i. *Cream-jug. Height* $3\frac{1}{4}$ *in. About* 1760.
ii. *Teapot, painted by David Rhodes.*
Reverse shown on Pl. 16A, i. *Height* 6 *in. About* 1760.
Donald Towner. Page 31.

collectors of Leeds pottery. It contains twenty plates which illustrate by photogravure process a large number of pieces of Leeds ware from the collections which were then being formed, and although some of Kidson's statements are misleading, the book did more to raise the Leeds Pottery to the degree of estimation that it deserves than anything that preceded it.

On pages 14 and 15 of *The Leeds Old Pottery* Kidson says, 'It is stated in the various books relating to the history of the manufacture of English Pottery that the Leeds Pottery was founded in 1760 by two brothers named Green, but how this definite date is arrived at there is no information.' The same dissatisfaction with the date has been felt by all past writers on the Leeds Pottery, and for the very same reason. There is no doubt that the origin of this date for the foundation of the Pottery was, as we have seen, based on the reply given in 1854 by Mr William Warburton, in answer to questions put to him by Mr Thomas Wilson of Leeds, and contained in one of the letters just quoted (page 3). Unfortunately this date is unsupported by any documentary evidence, and before accepting it as authentic it may be as well to examine certain other sources of evidence.

Jewitt in the first edition of his *Ceramic Art of Great Britain* states that a wagon-way was laid through the Leeds Pottery in 1758 and that the Pottery was paid seven pounds a year and an abatement in the price of coal as compensation for this privilege. From these facts Jewitt deduces that the Pottery was being worked before 1758, and this is undoubtedly the origin of Lady Schreiber's statement that the Leeds Pottery was founded in 1758. Since Jewitt omits any mention of this wagon-way in the second edition of his book, it seemed necessary that his statement should be verified, and after considerable research the following facts came to light.

In about 1740 Mr Charles Brandling, Lord of the Manor of Middleton, a village about two and a half miles south of the Leeds Pottery, discovered coal on his land and started an opencast colliery. His agent was Richard Humble, who later became one of the principal partners in the Leeds Pottery. In 1749 Brandling began to acquire land between the colliery and a field known as Casson Close, near the bridge over the River Aire at Leeds, with the intention of laying a wagon-way or what might be described as a horse-drawn railway to convey coal from the colliery to Brandling's coal staithe at Casson Close, whence it could be collected for sale in Leeds. The construction of the railway was started in 1757 and it was opened in September 1758. Nineteenth-century maps of the district show the railway as passing through the Leeds Pottery with the main Pottery buildings on the west side of it and a flint mill, partners' houses, other dwellings belonging to the Pottery, as well

as an area marked 'Pottery Fields' on the east side (Fig. 1). The agreements
made between Brandling and the various landowners through whose grounds the
railway was laid were ratified by an Act of Parliament (31 Geo. II, Cap. 22), which
received Royal Assent on 9 June 1758. The wagon-way became known as the
Middleton Colliery Railway and the trucks were eventually drawn by steam
engines. The railway is still working and in 1958, to celebrate its bi-centenary, a
pamphlet was issued, of which there is a copy in the Leeds City Library and
which contained the above information. The Act does not give the names of the

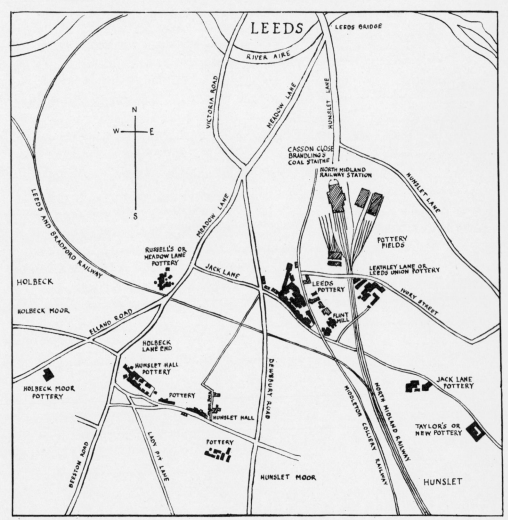

Fig. 1—*Area of 1 sq. mile south of Leeds (scale 335 yds. to 1 in.)*

landowners, but states that their indentures were lodged at the West Riding Registry of Deeds at Wakefield. On examination I found that one of these indentures (vol. B 3) had an important though indirect bearing on the Leeds Pottery, while a second also had a probable Leeds Pottery connexion. The first of these, which is dated 8 June 1758, concerns a close of land known by the name of Rushey Pasture which at that time belonged to a certain Jeremiah Dixon, and reads, 'Jeremiah Dixon Esq., doth Demise, Lease, sel and to farm lett unto the said Charles Brandling all that close of meadows or pasture ground with the appurtenances called Rushey Pasture containing 5 acres 1 rood and twenty perches, with, the stable or holm standing and also full liberty, for the said Charles Brandling to make, lay and place a waggon way . . .' (page 170). Rushey Pasture is again referred to in a memorial of indenture written in 1837 (page 171) and another of 1863.

The full text of this latter document is given on page 171 of this book and a part of it reads, '. . . All that close or parcel of Land situate in the Township of Hunslet in Leeds aforesaid called by the name of Rushey Pasture containing by estimation five acres one rood and twenty perches And also all that plot piece or parcel of ground being part or parcel of a close of Land situate in Hunslet aforesaid called the Windmill Close bounded . . . on the North end thereof by the residue of the same close and on the South end thereof by the said close called Rushey Pasture and containing by admeasurement and survey one acre two roods and four perches . . . formerly known by the name of one of the Dowbrigg or otherwise Dowbridge closes save and except a certain piece of Land containing two thousand seven hundred and thirty nine square yards being the North East End of the said Close of Land called the Windmill Close and which was sometime since sold to the North Midland Railway Company And also all and every the Buildings and Erections now standing . . . consisting of four Biscuit Ware Kilns, seven Glazing Kilns, hardening and enamelling Kilns, Brick Kilns and Sheds, Counting-houses, Warehouses, Workshops, Steam Mills, Flint Mill, Grinding Mill, Dwellinghouses, Cottages, Stabling and Land adjoining And also three cottages situate near Hunslet Moor All which same premises were lately in the occupation of the said Samuel Warburton and Richard Britton their under tenants or assigns but are now in the occupation of the said Richard Britton and have been and are commonly called or known by the name of the Leeds Old Pottery . . . And all other the hereditaments and premises granted and conveyed unto the said Richard Britton and his heirs by an indenture of the fifth day of June, one thousand eight hundred and fifty one. . . .' Signed 'Richard Britton.' The Leeds Pottery therefore was built on Rushey Pasture and Windmill Close. A

L.P.–B

further document of 30 November 1770 (West Riding Registry of Deeds, Wakefield, vol. BM.229/290) shows that in that year Jeremiah Dixon sold Rushey Pasture to Richard Humble, who, it will be remembered, was not only Brandling's agent at the Middleton Colliery but an early partner of the Leeds Pottery, his name appearing in a list of Leeds Pottery partners of 1781 (page 16). The document is as follows,

'Indenture between Jeremiah Dixon and Richard Humble. Indenture of lease and release bearing date 11th and 12th November 1770, the Lease being made between Jeremiah Dixon of Allerton Gledhow in the parish of Leeds, in the County of York, Esquire, of the one part and Richard Humble of Middleton in the said county, gentleman, of the other part, and the release being made between the said Jeremiah Dixon and Mary his wife of the one part, and the said Richard Humble of the other part and are of and concerning all that close of Meadow or pasture ground commonly known by the name of Rushey Pasture containing by estimation 5 acres 1 rood and 20 perches with the stable or holm standing in the said close which said premises are situate in the township of Hunslett in the said parish of Leeds and now in the possession, Tenure or Occupation of Charles Brandling Esq., his undertenants or Assigns together with the Appurtenances which said indentures are witnessed by Thomas Barston the younger in the county of York, gent, and Philip Coultman his clark.'

This makes it quite clear that before 1770 there was no pottery standing on Rushey Pasture, but that in that year it was bought by Richard Humble, who was one of the Pottery partners. On the 28th August of the same year, 1770, a notice appeared in both the *Leeds Intelligencer* and the *Leeds Mercury* stating that a large earthenware manufactory was then being built near Leeds (page 165). Although the date of these notices is about two and a half months previous to the deed of sale, this can hardly have been other than the Leeds Pottery, and it seems that Richard Humble, whose partnership probably dates from about this time, must have reached some agreement in respect of the land whereby he was able to commence building some months before the deed for the sale of the land had been completed or registered, a practice which I understand was not uncommon in those days. The question now arises—was this, in fact, the beginning of the Leeds Pottery? In view of the fact that a number of pieces of creamware believed to have been made by the Leeds Pottery bear dates earlier than 1770 (Plate 14), this is very unlikely, and the extensive building on Rushey Pasture in 1770 was probably an extension to an already existing pottery or new premises to which the Leeds Pottery was transferred. In the document of 19 November 1863 already quoted it is stated that the Leeds Pottery at that time was situated not only on Rushey Pasture but also on Windmill Close, formerly known as the Dowbrigg Closes, which lay to the north of Rushey Pasture, that is to say, between Rushey Pasture and Casson Close, which was a total distance of about three hundred yards. The same document states that part of the northern end of this area had been sold to the North Midland Railway Co. This further area owned by the Leeds Pottery therefore must have been very close or, in fact, adjacent to Casson Close, where the North Midland railway station is shown on nineteenth-century maps (Fig. 1, page 6). It is significant that an indenture of 1758 (B.3 West Riding Registry of Deeds) shows that a small piece of land in this same area, adjoining the southern end of Casson Close, was then leased to Charles Brandling by a group of partners in a concern the nature of which is not stated (page 170). Among the names of the partners given are those of William Green and Henry Ackroyd. The first document we know that gives the names of the Leeds Pottery partners is one of 1781 (page 16) which gives the names John and Joshua Green and Henry Ackroyd among the partners of the Leeds Pottery at that time. At least one of the partners in the Leeds Pottery, namely Henry Ackroyd, therefore was concerned in this piece of land near Casson Close as early as 1758, and it is tempting to assume that William Green, who was also concerned, was the father of John and Joshua Green, and that this was either the Leeds Pottery itself or land held for its building.

We will now turn to the third letter written by Thomas Wilson to Henry de la Bèche. This begins,[1]

Crimbles House, Leeds.
27 May, 1854.

My dear Sirs,

   In addition to Mr Warburton's answer to your enquiries I have gleaned the following particulars from Mr Petty, son of a Mr Petty who in conjunction with one Rainforth, an apprentice of the Greens, established an adjoining Pottery in 1757 . . .

The obvious inference from this is that the Leeds Pottery must have existed in 1757 for Petty to have established an adjoining pottery to it at that date, and further, since Rainforth had previously been apprenticed to the Greens, presumably for the usual term of seven years, it would appear that the Leeds Pottery was being worked by the Green family and perhaps others at least as early as 1750.

We must now consider to what extent we can rely on the statements of Warburton and Petty. Both men were sons of pottery owners. William Warburton was the son of Samuel Warburton, who was the proprietor of the Leeds Pottery at

[1] The full text of this letter is to be found on page 163.

the time that Wilson was making his inquiries in 1854 and must almost certainly have seen some of the early deeds of the Pottery, if not the original ones for its foundation, if such ever existed; and although the general tenor of Wilson's letters shows that Warburton took little or no interest in the Leeds Pottery of the past, and his answers to the questionnaire are extremely terse and uninformative, one would think that, apart from his father, no better authority could have been found.[1]

Petty, on the other hand, was the son of Samuel Petty, who became proprietor of the Hunslet Hall Pottery (Fig. 1, page 6), and the accuracy of his categorical statement that his father's pottery was founded in 1757 adjoining the Leeds Pottery cannot well be doubted.

A slight difficulty, though one which does not affect the main argument, lies in the word 'adjoining'. It will be seen from the map that the Leeds Pottery and the Hunslet Hall Pottery are about 600 yards apart and cannot be described as 'adjoining' unless the lands belonging to both potteries were contiguous, which may well have been the case. Wilson, on the other hand, may have used the word 'adjoining' loosely or inadvertently instead of a word meaning 'neighbouring', otherwise the inference is that Petty and Rainforth set up their first pottery very close to the Leeds Pottery—perhaps at the Leathley Lane Pottery, which is known to have had an early foundation—and moved to the Hunslet Hall Pottery later. But, however that may be, the importance of the statement lies in the fact that Petty and Rainforth's Pottery was founded in 1757, and that the Leeds Pottery was then already in existence.

In reconstructing the course of events from these documents and evidences there would seem to be greater justification for accepting the 1758 Indenture of William Green and Henry Ackroyd, together with Petty's testimony, rather than Warburton's unsupported statement. This being so, the following reconstruction seems to be the most likely—the Leeds Pottery was being worked during the 1750s. Its partners at that time were mostly men of humble status whose names are given in Document B.3 at the West Riding Registry of Deeds at Wakefield. The chief of these seem to have been John Armitage, William Green, and Henry Ackroyd, the latter's name also appearing in the 1781 list of Leeds Pottery partners, the others probably having died by that time. Henry Ackroyd, himself, died in

---

[1] The only record I have discovered that might have some possible connexion with Warburton's statement is a notice in the *Leeds Intelligencer* for 26 May 1761, in which Joshua Green is advertising the sale of four acres of land elsewhere in the neighbourhood which might have been consequent upon the brothers having become partners of the Pottery the previous year.

April 1788, his share in the Pottery descending to Sarah, his wife, and Mary, his daughter. The Pottery at first seems to have occupied a piece of land adjoining the southern end of Casson Close, near to, or probably one with, the Dowbrigg Closes, later called Windmill Close, probably from the Leeds Pottery flint mill which was discarded as such and converted into a corn mill in 1775, only five years after the extension to the Pottery was built and therefore unlikely to have been part of the new buildings. In consideration of Warburton's statement, the brothers John and Joshua Green may have become partners in the Pottery in 1760 though it was not, till 1775–6, that the name 'Green', in the trade name, was changed to 'Greens' (page 15). Richard Humble, Brandling's agent, became a partner of the Pottery, bringing with him some of the wealth derived from the Middleton Colliery. He bought Rushey Pasture from Jeremiah Dixon in 1770, upon which land the large extention to the Pottery was built in the self-same year.

This reconstruction of the early history of the Leeds Pottery agrees with both the documentary evidence and with Petty's testimony and seems to be the most likely one; but whether, in fact, it describes the true course of events in every particular, we shall probably never know.

CHAPTER TWO

History, Part II

HUNSLET HAS NOW BECOME incorporated into the mass of houses, streets and factories that for the main part constitute the city of Leeds, but during the eighteenth century it was still only a village, surrounded by green fields and open country. About half a mile to the north was the River Aire, on the far side of which stood the town of Leeds, which was then not more than a moderately sized market town. The road from Leeds to London passed through Hunslet, and in that area was known as Hunslet Lane, and we are told that along this road in the immediate vicinity of Leeds 'genteel houses with pleasant gardens lined the way'. Most of the cottagers in the villages round about Leeds were employed in spinning wool and weaving cloth, which was collected and brought into the town to be sold at the Cloth Halls built for that purpose at the beginning of the eighteenth century. But the rural and pleasant character of the countryside was already being threatened by industries of a more grimy nature than the spinning of wool and weaving of cloth.

A certain seam of white clay in the neighbourhood, which retained its whiteness after firing, had been used since 1714 for the manufacture of tobacco pipes,[1] and about 1740 (page 5) coal had been discovered near by. These minerals, together with a good navigable river near at hand, attracted an increasing number of potteries to the area. Of these the Leeds Pottery, as its name suggests,[2] was almost certainly the earliest.

We can picture it as it stood on Windmill Close and Rushey Pasture soon after the new buildings were completed in 1770. Six kilns were ranged along the side next to Jack Lane, with two more opposite and three in the centre (Fig. 2, page 13). At the southern corner of the pottery there was a large gateway, on the

---

[1] Ralph Thoresby in his *Ducatus Leodiensis*, 1714, in speaking of the Wortley Hundred says; 'Here is a good vein of fine clay that will retain its whiteness after it is burnt (when others turn red), and therefore used for the making of tobacco-pipes, a manufacture but lately begun at Leeds.'

[2] In nineteenth-century documents the Pottery is sometimes referred to as 'The Leeds Old Pottery' (page 172).

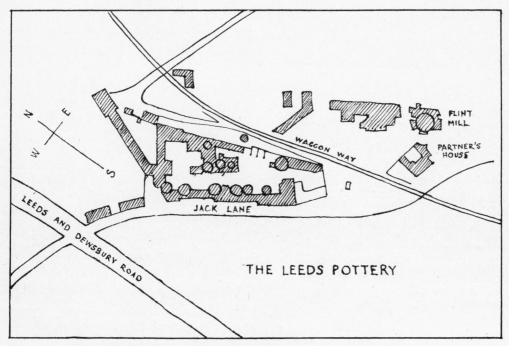

Fig. 2—*Plan of the Leeds Pottery (scale 74 yds. to 1 in.)*

east side of which stood a building with a bell tower, while a lodge flanked it on the opposite side. In front of the gate was a triangular open space where a weighing machine stood, and here Brandling's railway entered Jack Lane. Beyond the railway were some more pottery buildings. These included a large dwelling-house where some of the proprietors of the Pottery lived and was probably originally inhabited by members of the Green family. In later years it was occupied by Stephen Chappel and Richard Britton.[1] Close to the house was a windmill which till 1775 was used for grinding flints for the Pottery and whose position is shown in early maps by the inscription 'Leeds Pottery flint mill'. The name Dowbrigg Close was changed to 'Windmill Close', probably soon after this windmill was built. Its use as a flint mill was discontinued between 1775 and 1814, during which time it was used for grinding corn.

A short distance north of the pottery was Casson Close, with its great heap of coal brought there by the horse-drawn trucks along the railway track from the Middleton Colliery (Fig. 1, page 6). To the south-east lay the village of Hunslet; south-west was Hunslet Hall and the pottery of that name worked by Petty and

[1] *The Leeds Old Pottery*, J. and F. Kidson, pp. 15, 16.

Rainforth, with another pottery close to it. Slightly farther west, on the corner of Holbeck Moor, was the Holbeck Moor Pottery, which before 1769, was owned by Joseph Dennison (page 165). Two miles away to the south-east was John Smith's pottery at Rothwell. In addition a number of other potteries were to be established in the same area early in the nineteenth century.

In 1770 the Leeds Pottery was being run by partners who were clearly men of some culture and taste. We do not know whether William Green was a partner then,[1] but there is little doubt that Henry Ackroyd was a senior partner at that date. John and Joshua Green, besides owning a considerable amount of land apart from the pottery, had houses of their own at Middleton, Hunslet and Thorpe Arch. In a document of 1775 (page 15) Joshua Green is described as 'of Middleton, gent', while John Green is described as 'of Hunslet, potter'; and it may be that while John was responsible for the productions of the Pottery, Joshua was concerned with the financial side of the business. Richard Humble, as we have already seen, was Brandling's agent and brought some of the wealth derived from the Middleton Colliery into the pottery and purchased the land on which the large new extension was built.

Kidson tells us that the Greens also owned a considerable amount of land close to the Pottery on which they built cottages to house the workmen as they grew more numerous with the increasing size and commercial success of the Pottery. This would correspond with the area marked on old maps as Pottery Fields and included land both North and South of Ivory Street (Fig. 1, page 6). The Greens also owned the principal shares of the Swinton Pottery which was about twenty-four miles south of Leeds on the River Don (page 155) and for some time the two potteries were run as a single concern.

In the letter of 27 May 1854, from Thomas Wilson to Sir Henry de la Bèche (page 163), Wilson had interviewed a certain Mr W. M. Maude, who may well have been one of the potters employed by the Greens at the Leeds Pottery, as Warburton mentions that several were still living at Leeds at the time of Wilson's research. Maude gives the following information. 'About 1790 John Green had a quarrel with the Navigation about the dues on flints and in consequence had them carried up the Wharfe to Tadcaster—there by land to Thorpe Arch, where they were ground—and then carted fourteen miles to Leeds.' This information evidently gave Wilson the idea of going to Flint Mills at Thorpe Arch with the

---

[1] It seems probable that William Green was a partner at this time, as the Pottery's trade name in 1775 was Humble, Green & Co., Green being singular, whereas in 1776 it became Humble, Hartley, Greens & Co.

intention of searching the title deeds of the mills, with the result that he found an agreement which he quotes in the same latter (page 164). This corroborates Maude's statement except as to date. Wilson writes: 'I have met among the Title Deeds of Flint Mills with a draft of the following agreement—which I have no doubt was executed as the Flint grinding is carried on there to this day—

"1775 November 11

"Joshua Green of Middleton, Gent, and John Green of Hunslet, Potter, with divers others under the firm of Humble, Green & Co." agree with Hutchinson and Evers of Flint Mills as follows—

'Greens were to put up at Flint Mills and keep in repair a water wheel with all necessary machinery for grinding flints—the wheel only to be used by Greens for 13 years. Greens were also to find a man to manage the business and as much whole burnt flint as could be ground—and to pay 10/- for every 100 pecks of well ground and levigated flints, the workmen's wages not exceeding 3/- being finally deducted. At the end of 13 years Greens were to be at liberty to take away the flint pan and everything except the water wheel and cog wheel.'

It was after this arrangement had been made that the use of the old flint mill on Windmill Close was discontinued as such.

An incident connected with the old windmill is recorded in *The Annals of Leeds* under the year 1774.

On Sunday, 31st July, 1774, the sails of the windmill belonging to the Leeds Pottery fell down with a tremendous crash; which being looked upon as a judgment for desecrating of the Sabbath, the proprietors resolved that the mill should never be allowed to be worked afterwards on the Lord's Day.

Both the flints and clay were sent to the Leeds Pottery by sea and river; the flints from Sussex and the clay from Poole. Hutchins in his *History of Dorset* published in 1796 says that much of the Poole clay in that county was sent to Selby for the use of the Leeds Potteries. This was in addition to the local white clay used by the Pottery.

Between the date of the agreement just quoted, namely 11 November 1775, when the firm was 'Humble, Green & Co.', and 30 July of the following year, when the firm was trading under the name 'Humble, Hartley, Greens and Co.' (page 165), William Hartley had become a leading partner in the Leeds Pottery.[1] We are ignorant of his previous activities, but from the time of his connexion with the

---

[1] Note the change from 'Green' to 'Greens' in the trade name at this time.

firm the Leeds Pottery may be said to have entered upon a new epoch not only of increasing prosperity, but one which is evidenced by a complete change in the style and manufacture of the wares themselves.

It is quite clear that William Hartley very quickly took the lead in the affairs of the Pottery and that it was largely his drive and initiative that made the Pottery the great commercial success that it became during the last quarter of the eighteenth century.

There is no doubt that till about the year 1775 there had been little fresh development in the productions of the Pottery and, compared with some of the more enterprising Staffordshire factories, the Leeds Pottery may be said to have been old-fashioned, but from about that time new materials were incorporated into the creamware, due to the releasing in 1775 of the patent restriction on Cornish stone and clay as far as earthenware potters were concerned, and although this was no doubt responsible for a great deal, yet it is noticeable from the wares themselves that there was a new influence at work in the productions, and one cannot but feel that when William Hartley joined the firm he did so imbued with the idea of emulating Wedgwood and aspiring to a like success. Yet he evidently possessed too much character of his own to become a mere imitator of his rival, with the result that the Leeds wares, and particularly the creamware on which the Pottery largely concentrated for the next twenty years, though they showed the influence of the latest trends in design, still possessed a living quality, had every appearance of being hand-made and looked as though the potter and decorator enjoyed both making and decorating them; and it is these qualities that have endeared them to the heart of the collector.

The following advertisement in the *Leeds Intelligencer* shows that in 1781, Richard Humble resigned his partnership in the Leeds Pottery:

20th February, 1781

'Notice is hereby given that the Partnership in the Leeds Pottery between Richard Humble, William Hartley, Joshua Green, John Green, Henry Ackroyd, John Barwick, Saville Green and Samuel Wainwright under the firm Humble, Hartley, Greens & Co., is amicably dissolved and that the said William Hartley, Joshua Green, John Green, Henry Ackroyd, John Barwick, Saville Green, and Samuel Wainwright, will hereafter trade under the firm of Hartley, Greens and Company.

RICHARD HUMBLE	HENRY ACKROYD
WILLIAM HARTLEY	JOHN BARWICK
JOSHUA GREEN	SAVILLE GREEN
JOHN GREEN	SAMUEL WAINWRIGHT'

This is the earliest document in which the names of the Leeds Pottery partners appear as such. Unfortunately our knowledge of both these and successive partners is very meagre and the following account of them is largely drawn from scraps of information contained in local newspapers.

As already mentioned, the name of Henry Ackroyd which occurs in this document is also to be found in an indenture of 1758 (pages 9, 170) in conjunction with that of William Green and other partners in a concern situated on a piece of land adjoining the south side of Casson Close, and therefore in the immediate area of Rushey Pasture and Windmill Close, on which the Leeds Pottery extension was built, and although these partners are described as yeomen and small tradesmen, there is little doubt that they were the early partners of the Leeds Pottery. After Henry Ackroyd's death in 1788 (page 166), his share in the Pottery was divided between his widow, Sarah, and his daughter Mary (page 171).

Mary Ackroyd evidently became one of the principal partners of the Leeds Pottery at the beginning of the nineteenth century, as she, with Ebenezer Green, represented the firm of Hartley, Greens & Co. in the bankruptcy of 1820 (page 20). It is interesting that the names Green and Ackroyd, which are the first we know of to be connected with the Leeds Pottery, persist to the end. Mary Ackroyd married the Rev. Edward Parsons in 1789 (page 166), who himself became a partner by 1800 (Kidson, page 24).

Rev. Edward Parsons was born about 1758 and died in 1833 and was for forty-eight years minister of Salem Chapel, Leeds (Kidson, page 25). He married Mary Ackroyd in 1789 (page 166), and became a partner of the Leeds Pottery before 1800 (Kidson, page 24).

Richard Humble has already been mentioned as agent for the Middleton Colliery and the purchaser of Rushey Pasture in 1770, on which the major part of the Leeds Pottery was built. Although the document of 1781 (page 16) registered his retirement from the firm, on his death which took place during or before 1799, he left shares in the Pottery to Joseph Humble of Middleton and John and Thomas Humble of Newcastle upon Tyne, who were almost certainly his sons.

Joshua Green was probably the son of William Green and was John Green's brother; he may have become a partner in 1760. We find him selling land near Hunslet in 1761 (page 165), and he was a signatory of the document of 1775 (page 164) in which he is described as 'of Middleton, gent'. His name also appears in the advertisement of 20 February 1781 (page 16). He seems to have died in or about 1790 and left part of his share in the Pottery to Ebenezer Green, who was probably his son.

John Green was probably the son of William Green and was brother to Joshua Green. He may have become a partner in 1760. We first find his name as a signatory of the document of 1775 (page 164), in which he is described as 'of Hunslet, potter'. His name also appears in the advertisement of 1781 (page 16). He became a partner in the Swinton Pottery in 1787. He later resigned his partnership in the Leeds Pottery and became a partner in the Don Pottery, which was founded by his two sons John and William (page 163). He died in January 1805 (page 167).

William Hartley joined the Pottery in 1775 or early 1776 and soon after became the leading partner. He was married twice, first to Miss Booth of Park Hill, Bradford, in May 1777 (page 165) and after her death in April 1797 (page 166), to Mrs Hayes of Preston, Lancs., in February 1800 (page 167). It is clear that he had died before the bankruptcy of 1820.

John Barwick, mentioned in the 1781 document (page 16), was a surgeon of Leeds (page 171). He was also the Pottery's chief agent in Russia, where he was succeeded by his nephew Jubb (page 163).

Saville (or Savile) Green was a cousin of John and Joshua Green and was the Pottery's book-keeper. When the Pottery became involved in financial difficulties he went abroad and died at Rio de Janeiro on 14 July 1820 (page 168), a few months after the Pottery's bankruptcy.

Samuel Wainwright is described as of 'Boston in Kerseymere, printer' (page 171), which suggests that he may have been responsible for the transfer-printing done at the Pottery. After the bankruptcy of the Leeds Pottery, he managed the works till 1825, when he became the proprietor, and the Pottery then traded under the name 'Wainwright and Co.' He died in 1832 or 1834,[1] during an epidemic of cholera, at Hunslet. The document on page 171 suggests that his wife, Jane Wainwright, was also a partner in the Leeds Pottery.

Thomas Wainwright, who seems to have been Samuel Wainwright's brother, was the postmaster of Ferrybridge (page 166), and became a partner in the Leeds Pottery some time before 1783. He died in April 1798.

Ebenezer Green was probably the son of Joshua Green, as he was a devisee under the will of the latter (page 171). He was a liquor merchant and probably became a partner immediately following Joshua Green's death, which took place about 1790. He represented the Green family at the winding up of the Leeds Pottery connexions with the Swinton Pottery in 1806, and became a bankrupt in the firm of Hartley, Greens & Co. in 1820 (page 167), after which all connexions came to an end between the Leeds Pottery and the Green family, members of which had been its

[1] Jewitt gives 1832, Kidson 1834.

principal proprietors since its first known existence. Ebenezer Green died in July 1827 (page 168).

George Hanson was a merchant of Manchester and a partner of the Leeds Pottery in 1783 (Kidson, page 20).

Nathaniel Clayton of Newcastle upon Tyne was a partner in 1799 (page 171).

Ruperti is said to have become a foreign agent and partner at some unspecified date (page 164), and James Scott was also a partner (page 167).

It is unfortunate that not more is known about the actual workmen at the Leeds Pottery, but of interest in this connexion is a notice in the *Leeds Mercury* of 5 May 1804 (page 167), stating that 'on Sunday died Mr Matthew Wright thirty-four years one of the principal workmen at Messrs Hartley, Greens & Co.'s Pottery'. Wright would therefore have been first employed in 1770, when the large extension to the Pottery was built. An amusing notice in the *Leeds Mercury* of 16 August 1817 tells us of the marriage of 'Mr Thomas Craven a painter at the Leeds Pottery to Miss Coultate both of this town, after a tedious courtship of 28 years, 6 months and 6 days' (page 167).

From a personal reference to the Pottery's accounts, Jewitt gives the following particulars,[1]

In the year 1791 the yearly balance of the Leeds Pottery amounted to over £51,500, and in the same year the general stock was valued at £6,000, and the wind-mill at about £1,200. In the year 1800 the annual sales amounted to £30,000 and about £8,000 was paid in wages for that year.

In this connexion the following sidelight on the Leeds Pottery is recorded in a diary belonging to John Platt of Rotherham,[2] who was a mason-architect and also worked a pottery of his own at Rotherham which he founded in 1765 (page 170). It must have been he who made the valuation to which Jewitt found references, although the amounts do not agree precisely.

'1791

'19th Jan.—At Leeds Pottery, Measuring and Valuing Buildings, etc. for Messrs Hartley & Green, to 27th Feb. at ye Pottery, flint mills,[3] and other works there Valuing 34 days.

'10th Oct. Finished ye Valuation of the Leeds Pottery to Mr Calvert amounts to £53,860. 14. 8¾.
My bill and part Expenses £51. 9. 6.'

---

[1] *Ceramic Art of Great Britain*, L. Jewitt.
[2] From *E.C.C. Transactions*, Vol. 5, Part 3, 'John Platt of Rotherham', A. J. B. Kiddell.
[3] The flint mills were at Thorpe Arch.

In 1806 the Leeds Pottery relinquished its concern in the Swinton Pottery of Greens, Hartley & Co., of which it had previously held a major share (page 156). The signatories to this document for the Leeds Pottery were,

WILLIAM HARTLEY

EBENEZER GREEN

GEORGE HANSON

and for the Swinton Pottery,

THOMAS BINGLEY

JOHN BRAMELD

WILLIAM BRAMELD.

The Swinton Pottery continued as 'Brameld & Co.', and later became the 'Rockingham China Works'. The separation of these two potteries is an indication that all was not well with the Leeds Pottery. Except for William Hartley, who was still living, the men upon whom the Pottery formerly depended for its prosperity had died, while there seems to have been continual dissensions among the new partners. French privateers were rife at this time and ships destined for Spain or northern Europe, laden with creamware, were captured and taken to France. Further, the Continental factories were now producing creamware themselves in large quantities, thus depriving the Leeds Pottery of its export trade upon which it was very largely dependent. All these factors contributed to the general collapse of the Leeds Pottery.

Wilson, in a letter of 26 May 1854 to Sir Henry de la Bèche (page 162), states that in 1815 the estate passed into the hands of Assignees. This, however, was not the case. The bankruptcy did not take place till 1820. The *London Gazette* for 6 June 1820 states that 'Mary Ackroyd of Leeds in the County of York, Earthenware Manufacturer, Dealer and Chapwoman, being declared a bankrupt', etc.; also under the same date 'Ebenezer Green of Leeds in the County of York, Earthenware Manufacturer, Dealer and Chapman, being declared a bankrupt', etc. The actual date of the bankruptcy commission was 30 May 1820. There were a number of entries in the *Leeds Intelligencer* and the *Leeds Mercury* between 3 June and 18 July 1820 concerned with the bankruptcy of the Leeds Pottery (page 167).

It is clear that William Hartley was then no longer living, and except for Mary Ackroyd and Ebenezer Green, who were made bankrupt, the only other partner we hear of again is Samuel Wainwright, who managed to keep the firm working during this difficult period and in 1825 was able to take it out of Chancery and buy the whole concern. He worked it under the name of Samuel Wainwright

& Co. and engaged Stephen Chappell, who was originally in the cloth trade, as head cashier. Wainwright died in 1832 or 1834[1] and all connexion between the Leeds Pottery and its former partners was severed. The Trustees carried on the business under the name of *The Leeds Pottery Company* with Chappell as manager until 1840, when he bought the Pottery at his own valuation of £6,000. He employed Richard Britton as manager and brought his brother into the firm, which then traded under the name of 'Stephen and James Chappell' until 1847, when they became bankrupt. For the next three years, under the management of Richard Britton, the Pottery was carried on for the benefit of the creditors. In 1850 Samuel Warburton and Richard Britton bought the Pottery and worked it under the name of 'Warburton and Britton'. Warburton died in 1863, after which Britton became sole proprietor. In 1872 his two sons, Broadbent Britton and Alfred Britton, became partners with their father and the Pottery then traded under the name 'Richard Britton & Sons' until 1878, when it again became bankrupt. A copy of the Leeds Pattern Book has the following inscription on the fly-leaf: 'Received from Mr Routh the Liquidator of the Leeds Pottery Co., 20th December, 1878. (signed) J. Rhodes.'

At the time when Kidson was writing his book he tells us that the Leeds Pottery was a crumbling ruin; today not a vestige of it remains.

[1] Jewitt gives 1832, Kidson 1834.

CHAPTER THREE

Early Wares

THE MOST OUTSTANDING INFLUENCE on English pottery about the middle of the eighteenth century was that of Thomas Whieldon which not only affected the whole of the Staffordshire potteries but spread as far as Yorkshire, where white saltglaze, red earthenware, black earthenware, red stoneware both glazed and unglazed, and creamware of the plain, painted and colour-glazed varieties were also made, though the differences of local materials and techniques produced slightly different results. Most of these classes of ware were produced by the Leeds Pottery in its early days, a fact that has been largely obscured by its fame as a creamware factory.

DELFTWARE

Jewitt states that at one time delftware was made by the Leeds Pottery, and although this seems unlikely, it may be that delft collectors have not sufficiently explored this possibility.

BLACK EARTHENWARE

We are told by Petty (page 163) that the first ware to be made by the Leeds Pottery was blackware. This would have been the 'shining-black', or glazed blackware of the so-called Jackfield type, consisting of a brown earthenware body coated with a black lead glaze, but so far no piece of this ware has been found with sufficiently marked Leeds characteristics to justify any attribution of it to the Leeds Pottery.

RED EARTHENWARE

When we turn to some of the other types of mid-eighteenth century English pottery we find wares whose features not only bear a striking resemblance to those of Leeds creamware at a slightly later date, but which are absolutely identical, and must have been produced from the same moulds.

Illustrated on Plate 1, is a red earthenware mug in the collection of Miss Delhom of Chicago. It is of the type usually described as 'Astbury ware', which includes earthenware of various-coloured bodies which when glazed range from

22

3, i. *Taper-stick. Height 6½ in. About 1765.*
ii. *Teapot, 5 in. Height 4½ in. About 1765.*
Donald Towner. Page 31.

yellow or buff, through light brown, orange, red, to dark red and black, and upon which neat little designs in cream colour sometimes heightened with touches of green or blue mineral colours were applied from metal stamps. The particular piece referred to is of a true red earthenware, unusually light in weight for this type of ware, and slightly gritty to the touch. It has a reeded double intertwined handle, the terminals of which are in cream colour and from the same mould as those used by the Leeds Pottery on some of its creamware, and which are not known to have been used by any other factory (Plates 15, 27b, colour plate facing page 38 and Fig. 10: 13, page 153). Further, the shape is unlike any of the pieces associated with Astbury, but is found in Leeds pottery (Plate 37b).

Some pieces of this type of red earthenware commemorate the battle of Portobello which was fought in 1739; and although the style of the present example suggests a later date than this, it can hardly have been made later than 1760, and was undoubtedly made at Leeds, probably between 1750 and 1760, although evidence for the manufacture of this type of ware near Leeds, as late as 1774, is to be found in the advertisement of Samuel Shaw, who bought the Rothwell Pottery and made and sold 'all sorts of cream colour, *red, yellow,* and painted wares' (page 169).

WHITE SALTGLAZED STONEWARE

The class of ware in most general manufacture during the middle of the eighteenth century was white saltglazed stoneware, which was then referred to as 'white stoneware', 'white-ware' or 'common white'. We know from advertisements that it was made at Swinton, Rotherham and other factories in South Yorkshire, and there is good evidence to show that it was also made by the Leeds Pottery. A saltglaze sauce-boat is illustrated on Plate 5a. It will be noticed that it has a reeded double intertwined handle and terminals which are identical with those on certain pieces of Leeds creamware such as the teapot illustrated on Plate 32a (Fig. 10:17, page 153). It must not be thought that the moulded design for the body of this sauce-boat was peculiar to the Leeds Pottery. The same pattern was employed at a number of factories in Staffordshire and Yorkshire, and even porcelain examples of it are known. Unfortunately it is not every piece of Leeds saltglaze that can be so readily recognized as such, and there is no doubt that much of it is hardly distinguishable from that made by other factories with whose wares it is confused. The saltglaze jug illustrated on Plate 3 is a case in point. It is inscribed 'Success to Mr John Calverly of Leeds'. John Calverly became mayor of Leeds in 1773 and the inscription undoubtedly refers to that event. This in itself does not prove that the jug was made at Leeds, but it is most unlikely that a jug manufactured elsewhere would have been chosen for such an occasion. If it were not for the inscription, the jug might easily pass as a product of Staffordshire. Two teapots which are unusual both in their colouring and style of decoration are illustrated on Plate 4a, b. Depicted on one side of each is a young woman. In one instance she is seen seated at a table out of doors taking tea, while in the other she is depicted half length over a scroll inscribed with the words 'Miss Pit'. On the reverse of each of these teapots are buildings stylistically treated. On Plate 26a, ii, is shown a Leeds creamware teapot on which the identical young lady drinking tea and the identical buildings on the reverse are depicted. As this style of decoration, either in colours or in red monochrome, is frequently to be found on Leeds creamware, it is evident that the saltglaze teapots were decorated at Leeds and judging by their shape and other characteristics it is more than likely that the teapots themselves are of Leeds origin. This is further supported by the fact that 'Lady Pit Lane' (Pit also spelt with one 't') passed close to the Leeds Pottery and no doubt led to the residence of Lady Pit and presumably her daughter Miss Pit (Fig. 1, page 6).

Although a number of saltglaze pieces could be cited as having some Leeds characteristics and a probable Leeds origin, they are not included here, as the evidence for a Leeds attribution is considered insufficient; but saltglaze tea- or coffee-pots with a similar spout to the creamware coffee-pot on Plate 22b, ii, are thought to be of Leeds origin and acorn knobs (page 52) are believed to be a feature of much of it.

RED STONEWARE

A class of ware made in quantity by the Leeds Pottery was red stoneware, both glazed and unglazed. This, of course, differs from the glazed earthenwares of the Astbury type already mentioned (page 22). Vessels made in red stoneware are non-porous and need no glaze; the earthenwares are porous and require a glaze if they are intended to hold liquids.

Red stoneware is referred to in the Leeds Drawing Books as 'terre rouge'. A handsome piece of Leeds red stoneware is the engine-turned punch kettle and brazier illustrated on Plate 2. It has handle terminals of three patterns (Fig. 10: 11, 12, 15, page 153), all of which have so far proved to have been peculiar to the Leeds Pottery. Further it has a typical Leeds mask spout,[1] while the brazier with its pierced decoration has every possible appearance of being of Leeds manufacture. The kettle is engine-turned and is stamped underneath with an imitation Chinese

---

[1] The thickened part in the centre of the spout (Pl. 2) is due to a repair and is not original.

seal-mark (Fig. 6: 28, page 145). A number of pieces of red stoneware which bear this identical seal-mark are known and are of undoubted Leeds origin. The kettle cannot be claimed to be a particularly early piece of Leeds ware, since it shows a maturity of style that could hardly have existed much before 1770. That red stoneware was made before this at Leeds is evident from a red stoneware coffee-pot at the Taunton Museum which possesses a typically Leeds reeded double intertwined handle with flower terminals and a convolvulus knob (*E.C.C. Transactions*, Vol. 4, Part 5, Plate 4). This pot is decorated with small applied stamped ornaments which was the usual form of decoration on red stoneware before engine-turning superseded it. Engine-turning was first used as a form of decorating earthenware by Wedgwood, who introduced it on red stoneware in 1764–5, so that it would probably first have been used at Leeds some time between this and 1770.

Glazed red stoneware is at present more difficult to identify, but those specimens whose spouts correspond with illustrations in the Leeds Pattern Book are probably of Leeds origin.

CREAM-COLOURED EARTHENWARE

Both plain and decorated creamware were produced at the Leeds Pottery from its very early days, but as this kind of ware became the most important product of the Leeds Pottery it will be discussed in the two following chapters.

It will be evident from what has been said in this chapter that the difficulty of sorting the mid-eighteenth century wares into their respective provenances is considerable. This is largely because marked pieces of English earthenware of this period are so rare as to be virtually non-existent, the practice of copying styles and techniques so general, and the further complication that a number of potteries were then working whose wares are completely unknown.

CHAPTER FOUR

Early Creamware

THE CLASS OF WARE in which the Leeds Pottery particularly excelled and for which it became famous was cream-coloured earthenware, usually known by the shortened name of creamware. Leeds creamware was made from clay from Poole in Dorset, white clay from the Wortley beds close to the Pottery, flint from Kent and Sussex, and grit in the form of local sand (page 15).

Our present knowledge of the Leeds early creamware which is the subject of the present chapter is primarily derived from a previous knowledge of the later wares which were made at Leeds at a time when pieces were sometimes marked and records of it made in the Leeds Drawing and Pattern Books. Tracing back from these known pale cream-coloured wares to those made at an earlier period, similar traits and characteristics are found on a deep cream-coloured ware which often possessed the same double intertwined handles, flower knobs and applied terminals as the known Leeds pieces, and the finding of a marked piece (Plate 12a) in the earlier group has confirmed that the pieces of which it is comprised were all made at the Leeds Pottery. Kidson on page 62 of his book says: 'The Leeds teapot has certain peculiarities which are not found in those of other makers. The twisted handle is one of these, as also is the flower knob for the lid.' It must here be emphasized as strongly as possible that flower knobs and 'twisted' handles, as Kidson calls them, but which in this book are referred to as 'double' or 'double intertwined', following the Leeds Pottery nomenclature, were made by a number of factories, and it is no criterion that a piece was made at Leeds because it possesses them. It is true to say, however, that the provenance of a piece can often be determined by the particular pattern of such features, and the moulded details (Figs. 7 to 10, pages 147 to 154) are not only a help but often a deciding factor in making an attribution, though glaze, workmanship, shape and decoration and other factors must also be taken into account.

In some ways the early wares are amongst the most charming productions of the Leeds Pottery. They are rich in originality and good potting qualities often combined with delightfully fluent and decorative painting. The glaze, which is usually of a fairly deep yellowish tint, shows considerable variation of thickness. When it was applied too thickly it was inclined to craze. To obviate this, some of the ware was glazed very thinly, which gave it a dry appearance. Instances of this in the illustrated examples are shown on Plate 19 and the colour plate facing page 22. Generally speaking, the glaze covered the entire piece, though occasionally one finds examples in which the glaze underneath is so thin as to be almost non-existent and bare patches sometimes occur both inside a pot and underneath, but these must be considered as exceptions rather than the rule, whereas the under-sides of ware produced by some potteries, such as the Cockpit Hill factory at Derby, was seldom glazed.

At first saltglaze forms and devices persisted. Teapots had crabstock handles and spouts (Figs. 7, 8: 1, pages 148, 150), while the earliest coffee-pots and jugs usually had a strap handle with a pinched end (Fig. 7: 2, page 148), but new idioms were soon devised, amongst which was the reeded double intertwined handle with applied terminals at its extremities which became such a feature of the Leeds wares (Fig. 7: 5, 7, page 148). Sometimes the Leeds strap handle was also doulbed and intertwined (Fig. 7: 4, page 148). A double intertwined handle was also used by Wedgwood, but it was of a different pattern and was without applied terminals. (*English Cream-coloured Earthenware,* D. Towner, page 76: 3.) The Cockpit Hill factory also used it, but with applied terminals of different patterns, without reeding. Some of the handles made at the Melbourne factory in Derbyshire were, however, very like those made at Leeds, as indeed much of that factory's wares in general seem to have been, and they are no doubt often confused with those produced by the Leeds Pottery. The earliest Leeds knobs were either shaped like an acorn or a mushroom with a slight point on top (Plate 16a, ii), and unlike the Wedgwood, Derby and other factories they were rarely pierced for a steam-hole. Flower knobs were used a great deal on both the early and the later Leeds cream-ware, though the early types of flower knobs and handle terminals usually differed from those of the later period (Figs. 9 and 10, pages 151–2). One type of early Leeds handle was not only double but twisted as well like a rope (Fig. 7: 5, page 148) and occasionally one finds a spout treated in the same way. The cylindrical-shaped teapot, referred to in the Pattern Books as 'square' (page 67), was made at Leeds during both the early and later period, but most of the early teapots were 'round'. The early moulded borders of Leeds creamware were usually gadrooned (Plate 12b). Beaded borders were more general at a somewhat later date.

Creamware was capable of being decorated in a number of different ways. The early uncoloured creamware made at the Leeds Pottery relied for its effect almost entirely on fine form and good proportion, but moulded decoration was sometimes used.

SLIP DECORATED CREAMWARE

One of the earliest forms of decoration found on a number of different types of English wares consists of small patterns cast in metal stamps and applied to the surface of the ware. This is common on early saltglaze, red earthenware of the so-called Astbury type, and on red stoneware. It is also found on some early cream-ware, though instances of it are rare. Specimens of this are usually small in size and include teapots and cream-jugs. Two of the former are illustrated on Plate 8a. They are included here as it seems likely that they were made at Leeds. They closely resemble the early Leeds creamware and possess the same blemishes that occur on the early shell sweet-meat dish which is marked LEEDS * POTTERY (Plate 12a). Their execution suggests that they were pieces of a somewhat experimental nature, and in no way correspond with the sureness of touch of Whieldon and Astbury. It will be seen that the principal stamped motif is the same on each, so that they are clearly from one and the same factory, though in one case the motifs are coloured with a light brown slip whereas they are a darker brown on the other. It will be seen that one of these pots has a double handle which is also twisted like a rope and that it has beaded borders and a flower knob. Further the spout is of the same pattern as the small Leeds coffee-pot on Plate 22b, ii, and the spout of the other pot corresponds with a number of Leeds spouts (Plate 6b). While we cannot be certain, therefore, that these two small teapots were made at Leeds, the evidence is strongly in favour of such an attribution.

Another early piece of Leeds creamware in which a brown slip is used for decoration is a cow-creamer in the Keiller collection. This corresponds exactly with the early Leeds creamware in body, glaze and colour. The cow is uncoloured except for a patch of reddish-brown slip over each eye. The small square piece of the cow's back that forms a cover is finished with a flower knob of Leeds type. The plinth on which the cow stands is ornamented in the same way as the well-known small saltglaze pickle trays, though the particular pattern is unfamiliar.

COLOUR-GLAZED CREAMWARE

The chief form of colour decoration on early Leeds creamware consists of enamel painting, but coloured glazes were also used which followed the Staffordshire techniques.

Colour-glazed wares bear a variety of names according to their type, such as 'cloudy', 'mottled', 'tortoiseshell', 'green glazed', 'underglaze-blue' and others, but all are fundamentally creamware. These glazed decorations were popular in England before enamel painted wares became general, and were amongst the earlier types of ware made at Leeds and remained in production till the bankruptcy of the Pottery in 1820.

Thomas Whieldon, who gave the lead to this class of ware, was producing it as early as the 1740s, and it would appear to have been made in Yorkshire not long after. The first actual reference to its being made in Yorkshire is from Arthur Young, *A Six Months' Tour through the North of England*, 1769, in which it is stated that the Rotherham Pottery[1] was then producing white saltglaze, cream-coloured earthenware and tortoiseshell ware (page 170). Tortoiseshell ware is also believed to have been amongst the early products of the Swinton and Rothwell factories as well as the Leeds Pottery. The earliest piece of tortoiseshell ware that can be claimed as a Leeds Pottery production with certainty is the large punch-pot illustrated on Plate 10b. This is coated with a rich yellow glaze, inside and out, and is further decorated with manganese of a rather crimson colour, and a pale cuprous green. The moulded decoration is made up of a number of small motifs which are, in fact, the actual handle terminals known to have been used at the Leeds Pottery on some of its early ware. Somewhat paler in colour and therefore of a slightly later date is the teapot and cream-jug shown on Plate 8b. The stripes are of a crimsonish manganese, light cuprous green and deep yellow. These colours, with the addition of an indigo blue, are characteristic of Leeds colour-glazed wares and are to be found on the sauce-boat (Plate 5b) which shows the fully developed Leeds style of handle and the moulded 'feather' border. This last was also used by Wedgwood and others and was copied from silver. The teapot on Plate 9a is another example.

Between the years 1760 and 1766 Wedgwood was producing his green-glazed, cauliflower and other colour-glazed wares. He obtained his copper scales for producing his green glaze from Robinson and Rhodes of Leeds, and also sold some of the completed wares back to this firm of enamellers,[2] so that it is not surprising to find the Leeds Pottery imitating them, in common with the Swinton and other potteries. The two teapots illustrated on Plate 6 are clearly of Leeds origin. Plate 6a is of a yellower green than Wedgwood's ware of that type; and the handle and terminals are of typically Leeds manufacture (the terminals should be compared with those on Plate 16b, i, and Plate 13a, ii). Plate 6b is slightly later, perhaps 1770, and has a rather heavy green glaze identical with that on a dish

---

[1] None of the products of the Rotherham Pottery has yet been identified.

[2] *E.C.C. Transactions*, Vol. 4, Part 4, 1959, 'David Rhodes, Enameller', Donald Towner.

marked LEEDS ✳ POTTERY at the British Museum. Again the handle and terminals can be recognized as Leeds. Cauliflower ware is referred to in the Leeds Drawing Books and some shards taken from the Leeds Pottery site and presented to the Yorkshire Museum by Kidson are described by him as cauliflower ware. On examination they seem to be part of a mould for a cabbage or cauliflower sweet-meat dish. A cauliflower teapot and small covered jug in the Leeds City Art Galleries Collection, having ear-shaped handles (Fig. 7: 3, page 148) may well be of Leeds manufacture, and other pieces exist with marked Leeds characteristics such as the spout illustrated on Fig. 8: 3, page 150.

In addition to the useful wares, some creamware figures, decorated in coloured glazes, were made at the Leeds Pottery. The group of a soldier and a young woman seated in front of a background of greenery at the Victoria and Albert Museum can be cited as an example (Plate 11), as it is further decorated by a quantity of flowers, which are, in fact, flower knobs of the precise type that was made by the Leeds factory. The background seems to have been made from part of a dish. Related to this group is a similar one in saltglaze in the Willett Collection at Brighton. The group arrangement is the same, even to the little dog, but it lacks the extra floral decoration provided by the flower knobs. The saltglaze version was clearly made some years before the creamware one, as can be seen by the earlier fashion of the costumes worn by the two figures. Both groups are of such similar technique that one feels that they are more likely to have been made by the same hand rather than one having served as an inspiration for the other.

Other Leeds figures decorated in underglaze colours are Hamlet and Ophelia (a pair), and some good figures of animals. Some of the figures decorated in this way were made after 1775.[1]

ENAMELLED CREAMWARE

The early Leeds creamware decorated in enamel colours is a large and important group, made delightful for us by the painting of Robinson and Rhodes and others. 'Robinson and Rhodes' was a firm of enamellers in Briggate, Leeds, about whom we have a considerable amount of knowledge owing to a correspondence they had with Wedgwood which lasted over a number of years and which has been preserved in the Wedgwood Museum at Barlaston. In 1760 and again in 1761 they advertised in the *Leeds Intelligencer* (page 164) that they enamelled, gilded, and repaired china. In 1763 Jasper Robinson gave up his share in the partnership, but continued to

---

[1] Most of the figures mentioned are illustrated in Donald Towner, *English Cream-coloured Earthenware*, 1957.

work as an enameller for the firm which then traded under the name 'D. Rhodes & Co.'. In 1768 David Rhodes left Leeds for London, where he worked as Wedgwood's chief enameller till his death in 1777.

This firm set a style to much of the Leeds enamelling which continued long after 1768, and it seems likely that from that date the Leeds Pottery may have started its own enamelling shops and have employed enamellers from the firm of D. Rhodes & Co., which presumably was discontinued when Rhodes left, though it may have continued for a time under Robinson. Some of the styles of painting executed by Rhodes at Leeds are known by the corresponding styles found on Wedgwood's creamware made shortly after 1768, though, with the employment of new enamellers in the London workshop and the necessity for meeting Josiah Wedgwood's wishes, the style began to show some variation and was eventually absorbed in the taste for border patterns. Much of Rhodes's enamelling that we find on the early Leeds creamware is in black and red, though flower knobs on tea- and coffee-pots and handle terminals were very often touched in with light blue, green, yellow and sometimes rose pink (colour plate facing page 22). Some of the best of this painting consists of figures, dressed in the costume of the time, with a landscape background. An example of this type is illustrated in colour on the plate facing page 4, where the deep cream colour of the early Leeds creamware is shown. Other illustrations of Rhodes figure-painting on Leeds creamware will be found on Plates 16a, 16b, 17b, and consist of men and women in shooting, fishing, and love scenes. Conspicuous in the landscapes are cottages, usually with smoking chimneys; windmills; flocks of birds and little clouds; a tree on the right-hand side with a crossed stem balanced on the left by a plant with corkscrew foliage; some strong horizontal strokes in black in the foreground, sometimes with some wispy downward strokes like grass growing upside down, probably intended for water with reflections of reeds, while some round objects may be intended for rocks or stones.

Another noticeable type of decoration by Rhodes consists of stylized birds (Plate 19). Noticeable in such painting is the use of a point to scratch away the enamel for the light-coloured feathers, and the use of a finger in the same way, for the broader light parts, where the fingerprint of the enameller can be seen.

Though some of the flower painting was also in black and red (Plate 17a, i), touches of blue, green, yellow, rose pink or crimson were very often introduced (Plate 17a, ii). These same colours predominate in a style of painting which Rhodes also used a great deal on Wedgwood's creamware and which was known as 'chintz'. This consisted of the intermingling of stripes, chevrons and other motifs, producing a very bizarre effect, which was nevertheless extremely pleasing. A Leeds example is shown on Plate 31b, iii.

Often combined with these forms of decoration were inscriptions surrounded by a cartouche of free and rhythmic scroll-work (Plates 14, 17b, i).

Robinson and Rhodes were not the only china decorators in the neighbour-hood. Two miles in a south-easterly direction from the Leeds Pottery, John Smith had a china enamelling workshop at Rothwell. John Platt in his diary of 1772 says, 'At Rothwell valuing building and stock of J. Smith ye Painter and three more partners of a pottery at Rothwell near Leeds, which they gave up the works not answering' (page 169). The advertisement for the sale of this pottery emphasizes its enamelling activities and tells us that it possessed 'three spacious rooms fitted up for enamel work', which sounds a great deal for a pottery of only three kilns, and it is more than likely that John Smith enamelled for other potteries as well, which may account for some of the enamelling on Leeds creamware of this period that does not appear to have been done by Robinson and Rhodes. Much of this enamelling consists of conventionalized floral sprays thickly painted in either green or purple monochrome (Plate 18a, b). The purple painting on the taper stick shown in colour facing page 22 may also be by the same hand, though the convention here is slightly different, and the enamel is applied more thinly.

Some superb quality gilding on Leeds deep cream-coloured ware was probably done in London at James Giles's workshop.[1] Other gilding consisting of gold leaf, much of which has by now usually been worn away, was probably applied by Robinson and Rhodes, as it occurs in conjunction with their painting.

[1] An example is illustrated in Donald Towner, *English Cream-coloured Earthenware* (Pl. 43b).

CHAPTER FIVE

Later Creamware

FROM THE YEAR 1775 a great change was noticeable in the creamware produced by the Leeds Pottery. It was during this year that Richard Champion's patent restricting the use of Cornish stone and clay was released by Act of Parliament for the use of earthenware potters, with the result that these materials were then incorporated into the body and glaze of Leeds creamware, transforming it into virtually a new substance that was both paler in colour and more brittle in appearance than the deep cream or buff-coloured creamware which preceded it. It now approximated much more closely to the pale cream-coloured ware which Wedgwood had been manufacturing for the last ten years and which he named 'Queen's ware'. It was the ambition of all creamware manufacturers at about this time to produce as pale a ware as possible, and Wedgwood, writing to his London showrooms in 1768, says: 'With respect to the colour of my ware, I endeavour to make it as pale as possible to continue it cream colour, and find my customers in general, though not every individual of them, think the alteration I have made in that respect a great improvement, but it is impossible that any one colour, even though it were to come down from Heaven, should please every taste, and I cannot regularly make two cream colours, a deep and a light shade, without having two works for that purpose. . . .' It follows that if Wedgwood with all his resources could not make both the deep and the light shade of creamware at the same time, how much more impossible would it have been for the smaller potteries to have done so. That the pale creamware succeeded the deeper colour can therefore be accepted as a principle. At Leeds the change was particularly marked and, as already stated, took place about the year 1775. The successive and finer gradations of tint that followed form a further valuable indication of the sequence in which the pieces were made.

Nor was the matter of colour the only change. New ideas for design and ornament had been introduced into England by the brothers Adam, and these, which we now term the neo-classic style or taste, were fast ousting the old rococo forms. Wedgwood was quick to seize on the new forms of design and

33

adapt them for the manufacture of earthenware, and other potters soon followed his example.

In this self-same year, 1775, or early in 1776, William Hartley became a partner of the Leeds Pottery and seems to have immediately taken the lead in directing the workings of the factory, and it was undoubtedly his modernizing influence that was responsible for the adoption of the new designs at the Leeds Pottery. In giving Hartley the credit for this new development, we must not overlook the fact that without workmen whose skill was equal to the task, the Pottery would have become both a commercial and artistic failure. Hartley was indeed fortunate in his potters, one of the principal and most respected of whom was Matthew Wright, who worked at the Leeds Pottery from 1770 till his death in 1804 (*Leeds Intelligencer*, 5 May 1804, p. 167). Many of the Leeds designs were derived from the work of the silversmith and one finds instructions in the early Drawing Books directing the potter to fashion his ware 'as done in silver'. Consequently during the period 1775–1802 full use was made of pierced openwork decoration. This was a class of work in which the Leeds Pottery particularly excelled. The work was sharp and clean, the arrangements and shapes of the piercing were ingenious and delightful, and the general pattern well related to the ware it decorated. Doubtless the pierced decoration also served the purpose of lessening the weight of the ware for export, which was taxed accordingly. The Leeds Pattern Book, now reproduced for the first time (pages 59 to 141), includes a great many examples of pierced ware, varying from very small pieces such as salts, strainers, and egg-cups to the magnificent cruets (Plate 21a) and chestnut-baskets (Plate 20a). Pierced work required the greatest skill and care in the making, not only to punch the unfired clay, but also to know and maintain the exact state of hardness and humidity at which piercing, whether with a punch or a knife, could be done without impairing the walls of the vessel to which it was being applied.

The old-fashioned shell-like forms now gave place to swags, urns, husks, goat's heads, and acanthus leaves. In spite, however, of the taming influence of the new taste, the Leeds creamware perhaps more than any other retained a great deal of its old vigour and originality. The wares were well proportioned and balanced, the ornament was restrained and a sense of refinement in the potting and design was never lost sight of.

Some of the wares produced by the Leeds Pottery at this time testify to the prodigious technical skill of its potters. Large centre-pieces more than two feet high, of elaborate design and intricate moulded decoration, made in several parts and complete with removable baskets and bottles (Plate 25); urns with refined and complicated modelling, made to be used as candelabra[1] (Plate 23); elaborate designs for tureens, cockle-pots and pot-pourris, often enriched with figures (Plate 24); were amongst some of the most ambitious productions of the Pottery. Engravings of many such pieces can be seen in the Pattern Book. Side by side with these extravagances the humbler pieces continued to be made with much the same artistry and skill as before.

CREAMWARE FIGURES

Apart from figures as adjuncts to the useful wares such as occur on some of the pieces just mentioned, and a certain number decorated in underglaze colours (page 30), the Leeds Pottery does not appear to have made many figures until the introduction of pearlware a few years before 1790, but between this date and 1800 a quantity of figures were produced. These were mostly in pearlware (page 44) but some were in creamware.

Uncoloured creamware figures made between 1775 and 1820 seldom bore a factory mark. They include the 'Flute-player' (Plate 38) and a version of Venus, which differs from the pearlware model illustrated on Plate 40 in holding the doves in both hands, some small classical figures and a large-sized figure of a horse (Plate 43a, b). The Leeds horses are referred to on page 45. Some creamware figures with the impressed mark LEEDS * POTTERY in small regular type (Fig. 5: 9, page 144) have been produced in fairly recent times. These are smaller than the original figures, showing that they were not made from the original moulds but from casts taken of earlier figures. The bases or plinths of the original figures are more sturdy than those of recent manufacture, whose glaze is greener than the original and is usually crazed. There are such consistent facial likenesses between all the Leeds human figures, particularly in regard to their rather snub noses and slightly receding chins, that it would seem that most of them were modelled by one man. This modeller's name is now known to us by the recent discovery of the inscription 'John Smith 1797', incised underneath the plinth of the 'Flute Player' at the Yorkshire Museum, York (Plate 38). The question at once arises—Could this be the John Smith who was one of the partners at the Rothwell factory, which was only a short distance away from the Leeds Pottery? John Smith of Rothwell was a painter who left the Rothwell Pottery on its failure in 1774 (page 158), and it is tempting to think that he was also a modeller and after the sale of his own works became both an enameller and modeller at the Leeds Pottery.

[1] Such pieces were probably derived from Continental models, though a Chelsea-Derby candelabra of almost identical design to the one illustrated is in the Jones Collection at the Victoria and Albert Museum.

COLOUR-GLAZED CREAMWARE

Mention has been made in the previous chapter (page 28) of Leeds colour-glazed ware. This in various forms, particularly that in imitation of tortoiseshell, continued throughout the Hartley, Greens & Co. period. The magnificent coffee-pot (Plate 7) in brown manganese was produced about 1780. It possesses many of the usual Leeds characteristics of shape, handle (Fig. 7: 7, page 148), terminals (Fig. 10: 11, page 153), knob (Fig. 9: 5, page 152) and spout. Plate 9b shows a somewhat earlier tortoiseshell teapot in pinkish manganese, with terminals of the period before 1775 (Fig. 10: 1, page 153). The small coffee-pot on the same plate (Plate 9b) is decorated with dappled manganese of a violet-grey colour, and was made about 1780. This also possesses a typical Leeds flower knob (Fig. 9: 4, page 152) and handle. A teapot (Plate 10a) of about 1780 decorated in the same violet-grey with patches of green and golden yellow underglaze colours has not only a typical Leeds flower knob (Fig. 9: 4, page 152) and handle with terminals (Fig. 7: 7, page 148), but also a spout identical with that on the transfer-printed teapot on Plate 36 which is marked *Leeds Pottery* in the print (Fig. 6: 22, page 145).

Generally speaking, the manganese colour of the Leeds tortoiseshell ware was often more crimson in tint than the Staffordshire glaze, though the coffee-pot on Plate 7 is evidence that the Leeds Pottery also used a true brown. The violet-grey seems to have been peculiar to the Leeds Pottery, as was also some blue dappled ware combined with bands of underglaze-green.

Creamware decorated with stripes of underglaze-green was produced in quantity at Leeds and is illustrated in several of the Leeds Drawings Books, from which we learn that it was still being produced at Leeds at least as late as 1804, although originally quite an early product. Although most of the green-striped ware found seems to be of Leeds origin, it was also produced at Castleford in Yorkshire and by Neale & Co., of Hanley, and by other Staffordshire potteries. The frontispiece colour plate shows a fine Leeds coffee-pot of this type of ware that was made about 1775, while the teapot illustrated on Plate 9a is slightly later. Plates of this ware with borders of the same underglaze green are sometimes found with the Leeds Pottery mark (Fig. 5: 2, page 144) impressed underneath.

ENAMELLING

Much of the Leeds creamware of this period bears enamelled decoration. It will be remembered that David Rhodes, who decorated so much of the earlier Leeds creamware, left Leeds to set up his own workshop in London and soon after became Wedgwood's chief enameller. Whether the firm continued to operate at Leeds after Rhodes's departure in 1768 is not known, but much the same style of enamelling persisted there for some years afterwards, and it may be that the firm of Robinson and Rhodes which became D. Rhodes & Co. in 1763 continued under its former proprietor Jasper Robinson. On the other hand, there is no doubt that the Leeds Pottery had its own enamellers soon after 1775 and may have employed some of Rhodes's painters, who had undoubtedly set the style for some years to come.

It was evidently found that a wider range of enamel colours became possible with the introduction of the paler creamware, and though as a rule the brick-red and black still predominated, the additional colours of green, blue, purple, rose and yellow were now freely used, sometimes heightened by gilding.

Although much of the enamelled ware consisted of teapots, coffee-pots, cups and saucers, plates, sugar-cups, slop-bowls, tea-canisters, mugs and jugs, one sometimes finds the delightful little screw-topped boxes most of which were probably used for snuff, but might equally well have held patches, sweets or powder (Plate 31a). It would seem that both potters and enamellers put their best work into these very choice little pieces. The mustard pot, surmounted by the typical Leeds flower knob of the period, and the shoe buckle, both in creamware, shown on Plate 31a, are also delightful little pieces. With regard to miniature pieces of Leeds pottery, one is so frequently asked whether these were travellers' samples that it cannot be sufficiently emphasized that they were nothing of the kind. Agents carried wooden boxes lined with velvet containing full-sized specimens to show as samples, and the miniature pieces are consistently referred to in the Pottery's order books as toys.

A style of enamelling particularly favoured by the Leeds Pottery was red monochrome painting in which figures, landscapes, and flowers predominate (Plate 26a, ii). This can be dated as having been produced during the 1770s by the costumes of the figures depicted.

Styles of enamelling at this period include some enchanting banded decoration in gay colours, usually a rosy purple with little scattered flowers between the vertical stripes or sometimes within the limit of the stripe itself (Plate 26b, 27b and colour plate facing page 38); closely allied to this is the style usually referred to as 'chintz', which can be seen on the cup and saucer (Plate 31b, iii) and a coffee-pot (Plate 29), to which has been added a sponged purple enamel background. The same background and flower painting occurs on the teapot on Plate 32a. Other styles include chinoiserie subjects closely allied to those used on Derby creamware (Plate 28b), flower sprays in various treatments (Plates 26b, ii, 28a, 30a, 30b, i), and allegorical scenes such as the 'Aurora' teapots on Plate 29b.

An Oriental influence also showed itself in some very pleasing Leeds painting in enamel (Plate 28a) and in underglaze-blue on creamware from about 1780 (Plate 27a).

With the development of the Leeds export trade during the last quarter of the eighteenth century, not only was the bulk of the ware shipped to the Continent, but much of it was decorated there, especially in Holland, where the strong religious and patriotic feelings of the time were reflected in the enamel painting on creamware. Not only are pieces of Leeds creamware found so decorated but also creamware from the Staffordshire factories as well. The colours used by the Dutch enamellers differed from the normal Leeds palette and consisted of brick-red, a pale watery green, blue, maroon, black, flesh-colour, and yellow. This painting can be easily recognized, apart from the style and subject-matter, by the matt quality of the colours.

A great deal of the Dutch enamelling is concerned either with biblical subjects or popular historical events. The Leeds teapot illustrated on Plate 33a shows Elijah being fed by the ravens and is enamelled in black and flesh colour, very much in the Chinese Jesuit style, from which no doubt it was derived. A great deal of patriotic fervour was roused in Holland by the return from exile in 1787 of Prince William V of Orange and his Prussian wife, and we find Leeds creamware decorated in Holland with either a single portrait of the Prince or with the double portrait of both the Prince and Princess (Plate 33b), with inscriptions of loyal slogans in the border. An interesting teapot with the impressed mark LEEDS * POTTERY[1] and enamelled with 'Our Lady of Kevelaar' (*English Cream-coloured Earthenware*, Plate 96a) is in the Leeds City Art Gallery Collections (Plate 32b). It has the usual Leeds handle, flower knob, spout and terminals. The Dutch painting on Leeds creamware was free and often amusing.

TRANSFER-PRINTING

It is probable that transfer-printing was first instituted at the Leeds Pottery soon after 1775, as it was in full swing by 1780, in which year an important Methodist conference was held at Leeds and numerous designs of a pious nature were engraved and printed at the Leeds Pottery for the occasion. Many of these are marked 'Leeds Pottery' in cursive lettering in the print (Fig. 6: 22, 22a, 23, page 145), and include a portrait of John Wesley, which it will be noticed differs from prints of the same subject by other potteries (cf. *English Cream-coloured Earthenware*, Plate 83b), and a number of engravings depicting the virtues (Plate 36b). A small

---

[1] The mark on this teapot (Fig. 5: 8, page 144) is unusual, as the type used is oblique.

4, i. *Cup and saucer. Height of cup* $1\frac{7}{8}$ *in. Diameter of saucer* $5\frac{1}{8}$ *in. About* 1780.
ii. *Teapot. Height* $4\frac{1}{2}$ *in. About* 1780.
Donald Towner. Page 37.

curiously shaped teapot illustrated on Plate 34a, which has a print of 'Abraham and Isaac' on one side and 'Hagar and Ishmael' on the reverse, is marked *Leeds Pottery* (Fig. 6: 22, page 145) in the print. A print of the 'tea-party' in red on a pot of the same shape is illustrated (Plate 37b, ii), while in the Yorkshire Museum, York, are two other similarly shaped teapots printed with cattle and ruins in a landscape. One of these is printed in black, while the other is in underglaze-blue. Both are marked *Leeds Pottery* in the print. Other marked Leeds prints include a bull-fight in black on a coffee-pot at the Yorkshire Museum and was no doubt intended for Spanish export; allegorical scenes, either in red as on the plate (Plate 35a), which bears the impressed mark 'LP' (Fig. 5: 20, page 144), or black as on the Victoria and Albert Museum coffee-pot (*English Cream-coloured Earthenware*, Plate 61); a view of Fountains Abbey, probably one of a series of Yorkshire Abbeys and one of the best drawn and artistic of all the Leeds engravings (Fig. 6: 23, page 145) (Plate 35b); and Masonic Arms (*English Cream-coloured Earthenware*, Plate 60). Perhaps the engravings of flowers were the most successful of all the Leeds printed designs. Plate 34b shows two examples, a teapot printed with roses in red and a small jug with a fine printed design of roses in black pleasingly coloured over in thick green enamel. Examples of Leeds engravings treated in this way are rare, but two other examples are shown in *English Cream-coloured Earthenware* on Plate 63a, b.

Generally speaking the Leeds transfer-printing is inferior to that of Sadler and Green at Liverpool. The names of the Leeds engravers are unknown but Samuel Wainwright, one of the Leeds Pottery partners, was himself a printer (page 171), and may have taken an active part in the transfer-printing at the Pottery. The colours used for the overglaze printing at Leeds were brick-red, jet black, purplish black, and after 1800, blue-black and grey. Prints of butterflies were used extensively for the covers of tea- and coffee-pots.

Transfer-printing on pearlware and nineteenth-century wares is described in the next chapter. Mention should be made here, however, of the well-known 'Prodigal Son' group of transfer-printed creamware. In this the prints are coloured over with enamels and some pieces are either signed with the name 'Greatbatch' or 'W. Greatbatch, Lane Delf, Staffordshire'. This is a large group and many subjects are included, and although only a few of these are signed by Greatbatch, it is quite clear that they were all engraved by him. Some of the teapots on which these designs occur were made by Wedgwood, others appear to have been made at Leeds, while a great many others are of unknown manufacture, but were probably made at one or more of the Staffordshire potteries. It may be that many of the teapots were made as well as decorated by Greatbatch, and that after his bankruptcy in 1782 or his second bankruptcy of 1788, the copper plates were sold and came into the hands of other potteries. Alternatively Greatbatch may have bought the teapots in the white from other factories and decorated them himself. But whatever the full story may have been, it is clear on comparative grounds that some at least of these pots were made at Leeds. The example illustrated on Plate 37a has the typical Leeds flower knob and handle with terminals as well as a similar body and glaze to many marked and otherwise known pieces of Leeds Pottery.

GLAZES

During this period (1775–1800) the Leeds Pottery glazes became much paler in colour in conformity with the new type of creamware now being made, although for the most part they were still yellowish in colour, differing in this respect from those used by Wedgwood, which were of a greener tint. Kidson, on page 52 of his book, says: 'An examination of the glaze itself, where it has run into some degree of thickness into the interstices, will show that it has a decided green cast', a statement which has been most misleading. This does not mean that the Leeds Pottery never used a green glaze. For an interval of about five years, approximately between 1795 and 1800, quite a bright green glaze was used, but was discontinued owing to its devastating effect upon the health of the potters, while before this, from about 1780 to 1795, a grey glaze was used which often had a slight tinge of green in it, but by far the largest proportion of Leeds creamware was glazed with a yellowish glaze, very like the colour of a primrose. This finds confirmation from the fact that Arthur Hurst, in the catalogue of the Boynton Collection, describes the colour of the glaze of each piece with meticulous care, and out of fifty-eight pieces of Leeds creamware described, fifty-four have a yellowish glaze while only the remaining four are described as having a green one. Most of the remaining pieces in the collection are of pearlware, that is to say they are coated with a bluish glaze, a type of ware that will be described in the next chapter.

CHAPTER SIX

Late Wares

NO BETTER GUIDE to the late wares of the Leeds Pottery under Hartley, Greens & Co. could be found than the Drawing Books of the Pottery itself. Most of these are now housed at the Print Room of the Victoria and Albert Museum and at the Art Library of the Leeds City Art Gallery. With the exception of 'Drawing Book No. 1' at the Victoria and Albert Museum, which was begun in 1776, they were all formed between the years 1792 and 1819, which is the last date recorded in them. Since the Pottery became bankrupt in the following year, they practically cover the last thirty years of its life under Hartley, Greens & Co.

CREAMWARE

Creamware continued to be the Pottery's chief production to the time of its bankruptcy. This is demonstrated by the production of an enlarged edition of the Leeds Pattern Book in 1794, and a still further edition, the watermark of which bears the date 1814, which only illustrate creamware. Most of the designs in this book were also published in the first edition of 1783, and though from the year 1790 or thereabouts other types of ware were being made in ever-increasing quantities, it is evident that during this last period of Hartley, Greens & Co. the earlier designs must still have been produced to some extent, though probably in diminishing quantities.

By 1800 the creamware was paler in colour and possessed a greater uniformity of surface and glaze, but was less sharply defined than formerly. New factory marks were introduced some time during the first decade of the nineteenth century (Fig. 5: 16, 17, 18, 19, 21, page 144), and some of the wares of this time, such as the magnificent large chestnut baskets (Plate 20a), which still continued to be made were stamped with the mark 'Hartley Greens & Co.' (Fig. 5: 17, page 144), and are therefore of this period. Earlier examples of these bear the usual LEEDS ✳ POTTERY mark, and smaller specimens are surmounted with a 'Ring' instead of the 'Fir-Apple' knob, Fig. 4, page 52.

Soon after 1810 some of the creamware had become so pale as to form a white ware. Dessert services in this ware decorated with naturalistic flower paintings in enamel copied from botanical book illustrations, were produced in the style of Swansea and other factories.

Enamelling at the turn of the century underwent a complete change, and though at first some charming spot or stripe designs and rhythmic border patterns were made, these eventually deteriorated into the nauseatingly pretty, tightly executed floral sprig and spray patterns which must have been produced in prodigious quantities and were the sorry harbingers of styles to come.

PEARLWARE

By far the most important of the late wares was pearlware. This was a form of creamware which was glazed with a bluish tint instead of the customary yellowish or greenish colour. The bluish glaze, because of its opposition to the natural colour of the ware itself, produced a greyish tint to which Wedgwood gave the name 'pearlware', though a ware of this description had been in production since the early 1740s, since a creamware punch bowl with a bluish glaze at the British Museum is dated 1743 (*English Cream-coloured Earthenware*, Plate 1).

At Leeds, pearlware was being made by 1790, and its first manufacture was probably a few years earlier. The ware was coated with a glaze which sometimes ran into thick globules underneath or inside a piece where it appears as a deep soft blue colour, unlike that of the Staffordshire factories in which the blue is paler and has a slight tendency towards green. The Leeds pearlware, therefore, by reason of this glaze appeared as a light bluish-grey colour and possessed a richness and smoothness of surface which was extremely pleasing.

Except for some large-sized ale- and puzzle-jugs of intricate design of which a large quantity seem to have been made (Plate 44a), most of the Leeds pearlware was confined to tea- and coffee-services, jugs, mugs, plates, figures and smaller objects generally, which include some delightful little snuff boxes in the form of a lady's head (Plate 31a).

From about 1790 a change in pottery design is apparent in the Leeds wares, chiefly due to outside influences. New forms for jugs, mugs and other wares were introduced. Particularly noticeable are some new handle designs. Enamelling, too, had undergone a change, and we find the beginning of sprig and spot motifs which were to run riot in the beginning of the nineteenth century. The neat little border patterns introduced by Wedgwood twenty years earlier were now beginning to influence the productions of the Leeds Pottery (Plate 44a, b). Scores of these patterns, which appear to be the pottery's own designs, are drawn and painted in watercolour in the Leeds Drawing Books for the guidance of the enamellers, and although many are extremely pleasing, there is little doubt that the real artistry was already beginning to give way before methods which aimed at quickness and cheapness of execution foreshadowing the rapid decline of standards in the nineteenth century. During the last ten years of the eighteenth century, however, the Leeds Pottery still maintained a high sense of design and craftsmanship.

With the introduction of pearlware the marking of Leeds pottery became a more general practice and was no longer restricted to pieces illustrated in the Leeds Pattern Book.

The underglaze-blue painting which was so pleasing on the Leeds creamware was also used to decorate pearlware, but in this Staffordshire patterns were followed in a bold but rather careless manner and a profusion of pagodas and Chinese figures with umbrellas was the result. A type of decoration that was also produced at Liverpool, Swansea and elsewhere.

TRANSFER-PRINTING

The first type of Leeds printing on pearlware was in black overglaze and was coloured over in enamel colours. The 'Vicar and Moses' jug at the Yorkshire Museum is a magnificent example of this class of work (Plate 46). The jug, which is nearly ten inches high, has one side almost completely covered by a well-drawn, humorous print in black of Moses conducting the Vicar home by lantern light and is coloured over in red, rose, blue, yellow and green enamels. On the reverse is the entire ballad of *The Vicar and Moses*. In front, just below the spout is a painting of the golden fleece, the arms of the City of Leeds, under which are the words 'Success to the Leeds Manufactory' and the initials J.B. and S.B. (now almost indecipherable) probably for John Barwick, a partner of the Pottery, and his wife (page 18).

A branch of decoration on pearlware in which the Leeds Pottery particularly excelled was printing in a fine rich tint of underglaze-blue (Plate 48). This was first produced at Leeds about 1810 and was very frequently marked. Leeds patterns in underglaze-blue transfer-printing include,

1. A folly or ornamental building with a waterfall gushing out of the doorway and men fishing.
2. A temple with a waterfall, river, bridge and a boat.
3. Swans on a pond, surrounded by foliage and a distant landscape.
4. Two cows in a ruined abbey or castle with a landscape in the background.
5. A cow standing in a landscape.
6. A Chinese temple in a landscape with figures of Chinamen.

7. A border composed of village buildings.

8. The Willow Pattern of which there were two versions (Plate 48).

From about 1815, underglaze printing in black, grey, brown or sky-blue was done at the Leeds Pottery by a process known as 'bat' printing, in which the designs were first printed on to bats of glue and then transferred to the ware. This printing is often finely stippled producing an effect of great charm and delicacy and continued to be done in a more debased form long after the bankruptcy of 1820.

FIGURES

The Leeds Pottery produced a number of charming pearlware figures, many of which were marked. Whether these were left in the plain smooth bluish glaze of the pearlware or enamelled in the delightful and unusual range of colours employed at the factory, they never fail to please. Quite apart from the glaze and colouring, the Leeds square-based figures are easily distinguishable from their Staffordshire counterparts by the greater depth of the plinth or square base upon which the Leeds figures stand. A further indication of Leeds origin is a tool mark which is sometimes to be found in the corners of the underside of the plinth. This is no more than a vertical scratch made with a tool to remove an excess of clay and so prevent the possibility of a firing crack, a little nicety which does not seem to have been used elsewhere. It should also be pointed out that in most cases the glazed hollow interior of the Leeds figures is visible from underneath, whereas with the exception of the Ralph Wood figures, which are unglazed inside, most Staffordshire figures are closed by the base on which they stand. The range of enamel colours used for the figures include, pale yellow, black, chestnut brown, pale peacock green, and rosy purple; the hands, faces and hair are painted in their natural colours and the figures were often further decorated with small spot patterns. Typical of the figures modelled at Leeds are those which represent eighteenth-century young men and women occupied with everyday pastimes such as hawking (Plate 39a, ii) or playing with a dog (Plate 39a, i). Other Leeds figures are the seasons (Plate 39b, i, ii, iii). Spring is represented by a girl holding a garland of flowers standing on a rocky mound, a form of base often used by the Leeds Pottery either with or without a square plinth. Summer is represented by a boy carrying a sickle and a wheatsheaf, and Winter by a boy skating. These and figures of musicians (Plate 42a), a girl with a hurdy-gurdy, and a boy playing a tambourine are particularly attractive. Venus and Neptune, Air and Water (Plate 42b) are other pairs. All these figures have an intimacy which is quite charming; they are small in size, and are frequently marked 'Leeds Pottery'. Whether male or female they all bear a remarkably strong family likeness and are probably the work of one modeller—John Smith—whose name is incised under the 'Flute-player' at the Yorkshire Museum, York (Plate 38a and page 35). In addition the Leeds Pottery produced figures closely similar to some by Ralph Wood and other potters which were probably all copied from the same originals. They include the finely modelled figure of Sir Isaac Newton (Plate 41), Andromache and Mars, (variations of the last two also occur in porcelain) but in all three figures the work of the Leeds modeller is evident, particularly in the faces.

The most important Leeds animal figure is the well-known large-sized figure of a horse. Most of the Leeds horses are in pearlware, though one of the four specimens in the Leeds City Art Galleries collection is in creamware (Plate 43a), and as it differs slightly from the others in having no harness and a much flatter plinth, was probably the prototype for the pearlware specimens. It is enamelled a pale brown, so that the creamware itself is only visible underneath the plinth where it is left uncoloured. The height of this horse is 15¼ in., and the stand is ¾ in., making a total height of 16 in. Plate 43b shows one of the pearlware horses from the same collection. This is left uncoloured except for the harness, which is enamelled black with pale blue rosettes, and the muzzle, which is in purplish manganese underglaze painting. The height of this horse is 14¾ in. and the stand is 1¾ in., making a total of 16½ in. The differences in size which occur between the two horses are due to the different shrinkages according to the materials used. No two horses seem to have the same arrangement of harness, which is an indication that both this and the rosettes were added by hand after the model had been cast.

It has been suggested that these horses are not Leeds figures, but were made in Staffordshire, but in view of the fact that some of them bear the usual impressed LEEDS * POTTERY mark and one at the Yorkshire Museum, York, has a painted saddle-cloth with the initials 'LP' in one corner, this idea is untenable. A Leeds origin is further strengthened by the fact that most known examples of the horse were collected from cottages in the neighbourhood of the Leeds Pottery. It is possible, however, that certain late examples, made in white ware with sponged decoration, though made at Leeds, may not have been produced by the Leeds Pottery, but close by at Marsden's Pottery, Bedford Row, Hunslet (*Leeds Old Pottery*, Kidson, page 113).

Although much artistry, taste, and craftsmanship is apparent in the Leeds pearlware, by the turn of the century a great change was taking place and innumerable ingenious devices began to supplant the older forms of decoration.

WARES PAINTED IN MINERAL COLOURS

Differing slightly from pearlware was a whitish-coloured ware, very light in weight, glazed with a greyish green tint, and decorated with sprigs, sprays and border patterns painted in underglaze mineral colours of ochre, deep blue, brown and sage green. This type of ware was made by a number of factories, but the Leeds specimens are distinguishable from those of other factories by their remarkably light weight and precise painting. Many designs for this type of ware, painted in water-colour, are depicted in the Leeds Drawing Books.

BLACKWARE

Next in importance to pearlware among the late wares of the Pottery was the unglazed black stoneware, referred to in the Leeds Pattern and Drawing Books as 'Egyptian Black' or 'Blackware'. It has been claimed that blackware was the first product of the Leeds Pottery (page 163), but if this were so it would have been the black earthenware of the Jackfield type. The black stoneware produced by the Leeds Pottery dates from about 1800 and was an unglazed stoneware which was black throughout the body, and was derived from the so-called 'Black Basalt' of Josiah Wedgwood and other Staffordshire potters. Owing to its comparatively late introduction at Leeds, its moulded designs and shapes differ from those of the earlier makers, but closely resemble those in general manufacture at the beginning of the nineteenth century, and particularly those of the Swinton and Castleford factories, with which the Leeds Pottery was closely associated. On the other hand, Leeds engine-turned pieces more nearly resembled some of Wedgwood's basalt-ware, though usually falling somewhat short of it in quality.

Amongst the Leeds Pottery Drawing Books in the Library at the Leeds City Art Gallery is one entitled *Drawing Book for Black Ware*. It is dated 1800 and must have been formed soon after the commencement of the manufacture of this type of ware at Leeds, as the designs illustrated are numbered from one to ninety and the Pottery's greatest output of it seems to have been between the years 1800 and 1814. Hundreds of moulds for blackware which were taken from the Leeds Pottery are now in the Leeds City collection. They are mostly small and were for repeat patterns, borders and other ornaments. Kidson illustrates a number of these on Plate 20 of his book, some of which bear inscriptions, such as 'Working block; coffee pots; December 17, 1814', and 'For Black Egyptian ware butter-pot bottoms'.

The Leeds blackware consisted for the most part of tea- and coffee-sets, and there seems to be no evidence that the manufacture extended to purely ornamental pieces. There is some doubt whether the small blackware portrait medallions impressed LEEDS * POTTERY that are sometimes found today were ever made by the original Pottery.

Some of the details shown in the *Drawing Book for Black Ware* at the Leeds City Art Gallery include a 'lion', 'swan' and a 'lap-dog' knob (Fig. 3, page 50). But by far the most usual form of knob on Leeds blackware is the 'widow with her barrel', of which variations were also made by many other potteries.

The close relationship between the Leeds and Swinton Potteries is again exemplified by notes written in red ink in the *Drawing Book for Black Ware* under numbers four to seventeen. These indicate the corresponding number in the Swinton Drawing Book. Thus under No. 4 is written Swinton No. 5; under No. 5—Swinton No. 9, and so on. Written under some of the other drawings are the words 'from Staffordshire'.

Much of the Leeds blackware was stamped with the usual Leeds Pottery impressed marks (Plate 45a).

DIP DECORATED WARE

A form of creamware was introduced by the Leeds Pottery early in the nineteenth century that was so pale in colour as almost to form a kind of white ware. It was decorated with coloured clays or slips which are referred to in the Leeds Drawing Books as 'dips' and judging by the very great variety of patterns of this kind of ware illustrated in the *New Teapot Drawing Book* (page 53), it must have been produced in vast quantities. The decoration itself mainly consisted of spots and stripes of various colours arranged in an infinite variety of ways. The teapot illustrated on Plate 47a, iii, is a typical example and is impressed LEEDS * POTTERY. The Wakefield Museum possesses a number of mugs of this kind which show how delightfully varied this form of decoration could be.

The dip type of decoration was used in a number of different ways. The so-called *Batavian ware* (Plate 45b, i) was dipped in a deep brown slip, reserved panels on the sides having been shielded in the process show as white shapes against a brown background. These contained decoration of either underglaze or enamel painting. The same process was employed for decorating some tea- and coffee-ware in pale blue either plain or powdered on a nearly white ground. Small chequered patterns were often used as borders to this type of ware and gilding was also sometimes added (Plate 45b, ii). Dip decoration was also combined with other treatments such as an *agate* ware formed by a dip of mixed slips; *pepper*, which is a putty colour peppered with minute particles of black; *shining black*, with designs painted in gold lustre; and *encrusted* ware, consisting of small particles of coloured clays fired on to the body of the ware forming a rough surface. Most of these types were bordered with chequer patterns and the lower portion of the ware was often fluted, but left uncoloured.

A small figure of Nelson, or some other hero of the day, was sometimes applied to ware the main body of which is often marbled (Plate 47a, i) or decorated with a dip of an orange-buff colour either plain or with swags of foliage or reeded bands filled in with green. Examples of most of these types are depicted in the Leeds Drawing Books. Many of these forms of decoration had great charm and were typical of the Regency period.

YELLOW WARE

Mention should also be made of ware entirely coloured canary yellow over the creamware. A fine coffee-pot of this description is in the Hurst Collection at the Yorkshire Museum, York, and though unmarked is clearly of Leeds origin. Marked specimens have been noted.

LUSTRE

Lustre ware does not appear to have been made at the Leeds Pottery until a few years before its bankruptcy, as it is not mentioned in any of the Leeds Drawing Books before that of 1819, which is entitled 'Enamelled Tea Ware'. Towards the end of this book lustre is frequently referred to, though the only grounds mentioned are those of gold and silver. The mug illustrated on Plate 47b, ii, is impressed LEEDS * POTTERY and is of a brown body completely covered with silver lustre. A marked dish at the Fitzwilliam Museum is a fine example of Leeds silver resist. It has a vine border and in the centre, trees, a gate and a bird.

Tinselling is frequently referred to in the same book, where various border patterns are drawn with notes written underneath each, such as 'Tinsell'd Border on Fawn Body, Silver lustre ground' or 'Tinsell'd Border, Lustre ground with sprigs, Cornelian Edge, Fawn Body'. 'Drab Body' is also referred to. The sauce-tureen and stand illustrated on Plate 47b, i, is of a fawn colour, with holly leaves enamelled in dark green, while the berries and border are in gold lustre, and a dish at the Victoria and Albert Museum is of a fawn or drab colour with a rose enamelled in black in the centre and has an edge of rosy-gold lustre which may be what is intended by the reference to 'Cornelian Edge'. From this it would seem that tinselling consisted of lustre either used as an adjunct to another form of decoration or in resist (page 53).

CHAPTER SEVEN

The Drawing Books

THE ILLUSTRATED BOOKS in use at the Leeds Pottery were of three kinds. First, there were the books containing skilfully executed designs intended for the use and guidance of potters and decorators in the factory of which specimen pages are shown in this book (Figs. 3, 4, pages 50 and 52); secondly there were scrap-books of collections of drawings by agents and customers pasted into old account books belonging to the Pottery, showing the kind of wares required; and lastly there were the Pattern Books. These last—which will be considered in the next chapter— were published books of engravings illustrating the wares made by the Pottery and were probably chiefly intended for the use of agents in collecting orders. Of the first class of Drawing Books there are ten volumes known, nine of which are in the Art Library of the Leeds City Art Gallery and the tenth, entitled *New Teapot Drawing Book,* is at the Victoria and Albert Museum Print Room, together with two scrap-books entitled *Original Drawing Book No. 1* and *Original Drawing Book No. 2.* These last three books are mentioned by Kidson on pages 45 and 46 of his book. They were then in the possession of Mr George F. Cox of Manchester; later they were owned by a Mr Allen, who presented them to the Victoria and Albert Museum. There are many points of interest in all these books of which the following are a selection.

Drawing Book No. 1 (Leeds City Art Gallery). The drawings are numbered from 153 to 273 which indicates that there must have been an earlier book. The first date in the book is 1786. Some of the drawings bear special references to the Pattern Book, the plate number of which is sometimes given in a note against the drawing. A careful full-sized drawing of the urn-shaped 'vase candlestick' illustrated in the Pattern Book (No. 116) and on Plate 23[1], is included, as well as a full-size drawing of a ewer and basin 'of a pair made for SVA'. These initials refer to either one of the agents or another pottery. Initials of this kind are of frequent occurrence in these books; for instance, against a mug numbered 178 we find

[1] The Vase Candlestick (Pl. 23) is at the Victoria and Albert Museum and has the incised mark. Fig. 6: 30, page 145.

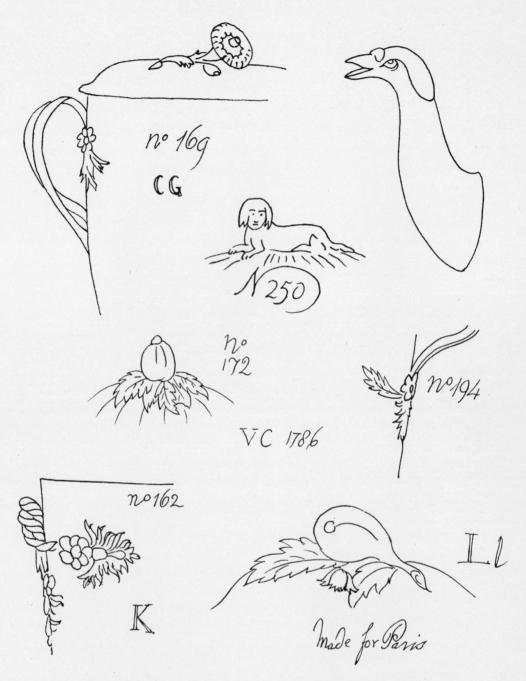

Fig. 3—Tracings from Drawing Book No. 1 (Leeds City Art Gallery)

'made for CP'. This might have been the sign for the Castleford Pottery, with which the Leeds Pottery had close connexions. No. 154 shows the terminals depicted on Fig. 10: 11, page 153, which are probably peculiar to the Leeds Pottery and were used by the Pottery more than any other pattern. The Leeds most usual flower knob with its characteristic terminal of two buds (Fig. 9: 4, page 152) occurs on No. 169 of the Drawing Book (Fig. 3, page 50). That a lap-dog knob very similar to, but not identical with, that used by Wedgwood was also used at Leeds is shown, not only by three drawings of it (Nos. 250–1–2) (Fig. 3, page 50) in the book under discussion, but also by actual ware impressed LEEDS * POTTERY. Numerous border patterns are shown in colour, including the familiar green and blue *feathered* borders. These, of course, were not peculiar to the Leeds Pottery, but were made by Neale, Wedgwood and many others.

Drawing Book No. 2 (Leeds City Art Gallery) begins at No. 274 and continues to No. 375. Perhaps the most interesting drawing in this book is the spout terminating in a head (Fig. 3, page 50). This is to be found not only on pearlware coffee-pots but also on pieces of saltglaze, though this does not necessarily imply that every pot with this spout was made at Leeds.

Drawing Book No. 3 (Leeds City Art Gallery) has the year 1814 in the watermark of the paper. It starts at No. 401 and continues to No. 457, these being all carefully executed wash drawings of pieces of creamware.

Drawing Book No. 4 (Leeds City Art Gallery) is unnumbered. It contains full-sized line drawings in ink one within another showing the various sizes in which pieces were made. The sizes are numbered 4, 6, 9, 12, 18, 24, 30, etc., the lowest number being the largest size. One of the most interesting pages of drawings in this book shows a number of carefully drawn knobs in use at the Leeds Pottery. Tracings of these will be found illustrated on Fig. 4 of the present book. These types are well known to collectors of Leeds Pottery, but it is satisfactory to have them authenticated in this way.

Drawing Book for Black Ware (Leeds City Art Gallery). This book is dated 1800 and is numbered from 1 to 90. Amongst the drawings for blackware knobs, the *widow* is of most frequent occurrence; others are the *lion, dog,* and *swan*. Numbers 4 to 17 apparently also occur in an unknown drawing book used at the Swinton factory, as against these numbers the corresponding Swinton numbers are written in red ink thus—No. 5 Swinton No. 9 etc. Other numbers have the words 'from Staffordshire' written against them, indicating the origin of the pattern. Many of the drawings show various patterns of engine turning (pages 46–7).

Handle Drawing Book (Leeds City Art Gallery). This book, though undated,

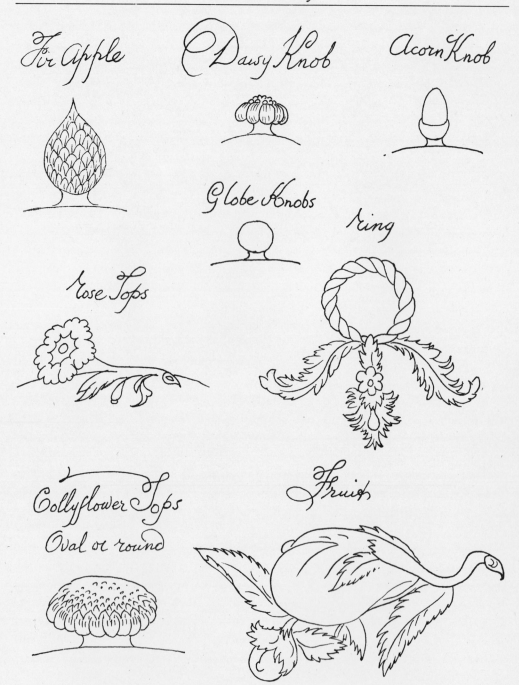

Fir Apple

Dasy Knob

Acorn Knob

Globe Knobs

Ring

Rose Tops

Collyflower Tops
Oval or round

Fruit

Fig. 4—*Tracings from Drawing Book No. 4 (Leeds City Art Gallery)*

was probably completed about 1805 and is numbered from 1 to 22 and contains amongst others the *Double* handle (double intertwined); *Common* or *Single* handle (loop handle); *Staple ring* handle (for tureen covers) and *Grecian* handle (for cups). A design of four flat leaves as a quatrefoil is labelled 'sprig for concave covers, either fruit, pine or colliflowr'd', showing that these types were still being made. Twisted and intertwined handles with accompanying terminals for chestnut baskets and other covered wares are depicted which are identical with those on Plate 20a.

Ornamental Drawing Book No. 1 (Leeds City Art Gallery). The year 1801 occurs in the watermark of this book. The drawings consist mostly of ewers, urns and bulb-pots. Against one of the drawings is written in ink 'Mrs Denby's Pattern'. There are so few records of the actual potters, enamellers and other workers at the Pottery that it is a great pleasure to find the name of one of them in this book, in this case almost certainly an agent, of whom there seem to have been a great many.

Enamell'd Tea Ware (Leeds City Art Gallery). This is dated 1819 and must have been the last Drawing Book to have been made before the bankruptcy in the following year. The drawings are coloured in water-colour and are numbered from 1 to 90. There are various written notes in this book showing that the borders depicted are intended to be applied to either fawn or drab-coloured ware or lustre. For example, one finds written—'Tinsell'd border on fawn body', tinsel presumably being a small design in lustre—'Silver lustre ground'—'on fawn body'—'on drab body'—'gold lustre ground'—'lustre ground with sprigs, cornelian edge', etc. (page 48).

Enamel Table Service Drawing Book (Leeds City Art Gallery). This book is undated, but judging by the drawings it contains, which are all conventional borders in water-colour, it would seem to have been compiled between 1800 and 1820, though Nos. 101 to 121 and Nos. 233 to 239 are on different paper and would appear to have been part of an earlier book.

New Teapot Drawing Book (Victoria and Albert Museum). This book is in the same category as those in the Art Library at Leeds; that is to say it is a book containing skilled drawings for the guidance of enamellers and potters working in the factory, and though it is not dated it covers a period of approximately 1805 to 1815, while the title suggests that there was an earlier Teapot Drawing Book. The drawings are numbered from 250 to 610 and are in pen and ink coloured over in water-colour and depict teapots, shown without handles or spouts, and various border patterns and other designs. Written in pencil against many of these, and now barely legible, are the prices paid for enamelling each pattern, as well as the number of pieces an enameller would be expected to complete in a day. For instance, one finds against one—'8 cups and saucers a day', and 'twelve in a day' against another; while the price for painting teapots varies from 1s. 4d. for under-glaze to 5s. for enamelling. One very elaborate teapot is marked 30s. That such high prices should be paid for enamelling at that time seems extraordinary, and one can only suppose that they are for enamelling a dozen of each pattern, which would bring the prices approximately into line with Wedgwood's, who, we learn, was paying his enamellers 26s. or 28s. a week at the time of his death in 1795.

A great many of the designs for teapot decoration consist of banded and chequered patterns in coloured slip, or 'dip' as it is called in the book (Plates 45b, 47a), the principal colours used being ochre, cinnamon, blue, reddish-brown and black. Teapots decorated in dip are shown with ball knobs, while enamelled ones are given the usual Leeds flower knob and terminal (Fig. 9: 4, page 152). Burnished silver or gold is sometimes shown as an adjunct to enamelling.

Towards the end of the book are a great many designs for decoration in under-glaze mineral colours of the type so often associated with the name 'Pratt'. These are mostly in ochre, green, and blue (page 46). In addition to sprays and sprigs a large number of border patterns are shown both in mineral colours and in enamels. These are inspired by the borders on Wedgwood's Queen's Ware, but few, if any, seem to be actual replicas of these. The patterns for some of the Leeds borders include oak leaves, strawberries, roses, thistles, harebells, and shells.

Other types of decoration include the *Moscha* pattern on a background of coloured dip; designs in *Queen's Blue Underglaze*; brightly coloured sprays of flowers for enamelling on dip; and at the end of the book are water-colours derived from the chapter tailpieces of Thomas Bewick's *British Birds*, as well as landscapes containing cottages and castles.

Original Drawing Book No. 1 and Original Drawing Book No. 2 (Victoria and Albert Museum). These consist for the most part of inexpert sketches pasted into old order books belonging to the Pottery. They are inscribed with notes in English, French, German, and Spanish, and appear to be orders submitted by the Pottery's agents. Each volume has an index of initials and symbols, presumably those of the firm's agents with page references. The only actual names of agents in the books are those of Miss Fenton, M. Jackson, and A. W. Hentig.

The earliest date to be found in *Drawing Book No. 1* is 1778, and the latest is 1791.

The drawings in *Drawing Book No. 2* range from 1792 to 1804. Besides being dated, many of them bear inscriptions indicating whether or not the designs were actually carried out.

Among the orders illustrated by drawings are the following—tea- and coffee-cups with black and white chequered borders, the bowl of the cups pale blue mottled with manganese, the lower half being either fluted or plain. A teapot of this type but without the mottling is shown on Plate 45b of the present book. An order for bottle-stands from Spain includes a request for each piece to be marked 'Il Tutto Marcato, Hartlei Greens C'. This is translated underneath by the Pottery 'The whole marked underneath Hartley Greens & Co. Leeds Pottery'. The words 'Hartley Greens & Co.' were subsequently crossed out.

There are orders for engine-turned redware—'en terre rouge'—with a design for chevron or diamond engine-turning. Some of the orders for 'engine teapots', 'engined bowls' or 'engine handled cups and saucers' in the second book may refer to blackware. One order is for 'Egyptian Black teapots with a figure on top also milk jugs in the same'.

It would appear that bottles with foreign inscriptions on them were painted at Leeds. One order asks for the words 'CUKIER, OLIWA, OCET, PIEPREZ, MUSZTARDA' to be inscribed 'all equal in size'. The English translation is written against each word in small hand-writing by the Leeds Pottery—'sugar, oil, vinegar, pepper, mustard'.

Creamware is illustrated decorated with green underglaze vertical stripes (colour plate frontispiece), as well as some with reeded horizontal bands filled in with green glaze on a creamware ground mottled with manganese.

Under a drawing of a butter tub is written 'the rim round the butter tub is to put ice into to cool the butter' (*Pattern Book No. 174*).

ORDER BOOKS

The order books into which the drawings just described were pasted are also of interest. A number of pages are not pasted over and can still be read. At the top of each page are headings describing the wares made, in the left-hand column are the symbols of the agents for whom the wares were made (these correspond with initials in the index to the order books), and against these and under the various headings are shown the quantity of each type made. There is often a general heading such as 'Candlesticks', followed by subdivisions, in this case 'Composite' and 'Corinthian'. Some other headings of the same kind are 'Toys', with the subdivisions, 'milkpots, bowls, canisters, teapots, coffee pots'. 'Teapots' are divided into 'plain, round, square', and 'sugars' into 'Plain, Dou: Hands' (Plain or with double handles). Written against some pieces are, 'Ordered at Swinton, to be marked etc.' or 'ordered to Hull'.

L.P.—E

CHAPTER EIGHT

The Pattern Books

PATTERN BOOKS with engraved illustrations and descriptive lists of wares in current production were issued in the second half of the eighteenth century by a number of the leading earthenware manufacturers for the use and guidance of Pottery agents and traders in England and abroad. The first creamware Pattern Book was published in 1774 by Wedgwood and was entitled 'A Catalogue of the different Articles of *Queen's Ware*, which may be had either plain, gilt or embellished with Enamel Paintings, manufactured by Josiah Wedgwood, Potter to her Majesty'. This consisted of nine plates of engravings depicting thirty-five different objects. These were described on a separate sheet and both the list and the book of engravings were sent out together. A much larger book on the same lines was issued by the Leeds Pottery in 1783, entitled 'Designs of Sundry Articles of Queen's or Cream-colour'd Earthen-Ware, manufactured by Hartley, Greens, and Co. at Leeds Pottery with a great variety of other articles. The same enamel'd, printed or ornamented with gold to any pattern; also with coats of arms, cyphers, landscapes, etc., etc.' A list describing the illustrations was issued by the Pottery under a separate cover and was written in Dutch, French and Spanish as well as English. Very similar Pattern Books were issued by the Swinton, Don, and Castleford Potteries.

The Leeds Pattern Book contained forty-five plates numbered from 1 to 38 and a further 1 to 7 for tea-ware, the designs being numbered from 1 to 152 and 1 to 32. This was repeated in fresh issues in 1785 and 1786, and in 1794 a further edition was published in which the number of engraved plates was increased to seventy-six, the designs being numbered from 1 to 221 and 1 to 48 for tea-ware. These illustrations were repeated in a further edition which is undated, but in which the year 1814 can be seen in the watermark of the paper. This last is the edition of the Pattern Book selected for reproduction and inclusion in the present book, as it has the advantage of including not only all the engravings from the earlier editions but the later additions as well.

The plates which follow at the end of this chapter speak for themselves, and collectors will be able to make comparisons between the engravings and actual specimens of creamware as well as with the illustrations at the end of this book.

The following brief notes on the illustrations to the Pattern Book may be of interest.

The first ten numbers clearly illustrate the patterns known as 'Feather', 'Royal', 'Queen's' and 'Shell Edge'.

No. 12 'Sea Shell' illustrates the early deep cream specimen shown on Plate 12a, which is the earliest known piece to have been impressed with the Leeds Pottery mark (Fig. 5: 1, page 144).

No. 38 'Triangular Royal Compotier' is shown on Plate 20b, and is impressed with the mark (Fig. 5: 2, page 144).

Nos. 42 and 44 'Pierced Desert Plate' are shown on Plate 20b. Both have the impressed mark (Fig. 5: 7, page 144).

Nos. 61 and 62 illustrate the double handle shown on Fig. 7: 8, page 148.

Nos. 64 to 67 illustrate the double handle shown on Fig. 7: 9, page 148.

No. 68 'Melon Terrine and Spoon' is shown with enamel decoration on Plate 28a.

No. 106 'Grand Platt Menage'. It is interesting to compare this design with a somewhat similar one in Wedgwood's Queen's Ware Pattern Book.

No. 108 'Dolphin candlestick'. A specimen of this candlestick is illustrated on Plate 21b.

No. 113 'Griffin candlestick'. An example of this is shown on Plate 21b.

No. 116 'Vase candlestick'. An example of this candlestick at the Victoria and Albert Museum (Plate 23) has an incised LP mark in monogram (Fig. 6: 30, page 145).

No. 137 'Chestnut Basket and Stand' (Plate 20a). The large-sized chestnut baskets had a 'fir apple' knob, while the smaller ones had a 'ring' handle (Fig. 4, page 52).

No. 139 'Cockle Pot or Potpouri'. The example of this shown on Plate 24 has the impressed mark (Fig. 5: 10, page 144). These large and handsome pieces were made with two covers, a plain inner cover and an elaborate outer cover. The cockle pot on Plate 24 has the inner cover only. Of the only two other cockle pots known to the author, one is at the Yorkshire Museum, York, while the other is impressed LP (Fig. 6: 30, page 145), but the design of these last differs from that shown in the Pattern Book.

No. 142 'Quintal Flower Horn'. Specimens of this pattern impressed with mark (Fig. 5: 2, page 144) are in the author's collection.

No. 170 'Double Concave Sauceboat and Stand'. The example shown on Plate 22b has the impressed mark (Fig. 5: 2, page 144).

No. 174 'Oval Butter Tub and Fast Stand'. This is also illustrated in *Drawing Book No. 2* at the Victoria and Albert Museum and has the following explanation written below it: 'The rim round the Butter Tub is to put ice into to cool the butter.'

DESIGNS

OF

SUNDRY ARTICLES

OF

Queen's or Cream-colour'd Earthen-Ware,

MANUFACTURED BY

HARTLEY, GREENS, and Co.

AT

Leeds Pottery:

WITH

A GREAT VARIETY OF OTHER ARTICLES.

THE SAME ENAMEL'D, PRINTED OR ORNAMENTED WITH GOLD TO ANY
PATTERN; ALSO WITH COATS OF ARMS, CYPHERS,
LANDSCAPES, &c., &c.

LEEDS.

EXPLANATION of the PLATES.

Reference to each.

No.

1 Oval Feather

2   Royal

3   Queen's   Terrines, from 7 to 14 Inches.

4   Shell Edge

5 Oval Feather

6   Royal

7   Shell Edge   Sauce Terrines, Spoons, and Stands, from 4 to 7 Inches.

8   Queen's

9   Feather

10   Royal   Ditto   ditto   with fast Stands, 5 and 6 Inches.

11 Pickle Leaf,

12 Sea Shell,   from 4 to 9 Inches.

13 Escollop Shell,

14 Queen's

15 Feather

16 Shell Edge   Sauce Boats, from 4 to 7 Inches and a Half.

17 Royal

18 Oval Royal

19   Feather   Dishes, from 6 to 20 Inches.
                   Round Dishes of the same Patterns, from 10 to 19 Inches.

20   Queen's

21   Shell Edge

Also Soup Dishes, each Pattern, round or oval, from 10 to 18 Inches.

22 Queen's

23 Feather   Table Plates, 9½ Inches.
                Soup ditto same Size.

24 Shell Edge   Smaller ditto called Twiflers, 6, 7, 8, and 9 Inches.

25 Royal

No.

26 Oval Queen's

27   Feather   Covered or Ragou Dishes, from 10 to 15 Inches.

28   Shell Edge   Round   ditto   from 10 to 14 Inches.

29   Royal

30   Queen's

31   Feather   Sallads, from 6 to 14 Inches.

32   Shell Edge   Round ditto the same.

33   Royal

34 Square Royal Sallad, from 6 to 14 Inches.

35   Turtle Dish, from 8 to 13 Inches.

36   Royal

37   Feather

38 Triangular Royal   Compotiers, from 7 to 12 Inches.

39   Feather

40 Round Feather

41   Queen's

42   Royal   Pierced Desert Plates, from 6 to 10 Inches.

43   Shell Edge

44   Royal deep

45 Oval

46 Round   Feather pierced Desert Dishes, from 8 to 11 Inches.

47 Round

48 Oval   Fish Drainers for Dishes, from 10 to 20 Inches.

49 Oval Royal

50   Pierced

51   Queen's   Salts, 3 Inches.

52   Pierced   The same without Covers.

53   Feather

54   Pierced

No.

55 Plain

56 Fluted and pierced } Egg Cups.

57 Pierced

58 Pierced double Salts.

59   ditto with Covers.

60 Plain Jug, from $\frac{1}{2}$ Pint to 12 Pints.

61 Fluted ditto,   ditto   ditto.

62 Round Plain Salt.

63   ditto, with Feet.

64 Fluted Cover'd } Mugs, from $\frac{1}{2}$ Pints to 4 Pints.

65 Plain Cover'd

66 Fluted } Mugs, from $\frac{1}{4}$ Pints to 4 Pints.

67 Plain

68 Melon Terrine and Spoon, from 4 to 12 Inches.

69 Round Terrine and Stand, from 6 to 12 Inches.

70 Handled Cover'd Bowl, from $\frac{1}{4}$ Pints to 8 Pints.

71 Cover'd Bowl, without Handles, from $\frac{1}{2}$ Pints to 8 Pints.

72 Cover'd Desert, from 6 to 12 Inches.

73   Ditto, with Partitions, 8 to 10 Inches.—A. The Cover.

74 Oval Queen's

75 Oval Feather } Butter Tubs, and Stands, from 4 to 6 Inches.

76 Oval Royal

The same, with pierced Covers.

77 Hexagon

78 Round fluted } Butter Tubs and Stands, from 5 to $3\frac{1}{2}$ Inches

79 Round plain

80 Pepper or Sugar

81 Mustard } Castors.

82 Oil and Vinegar

No.

83 . Round fluted ⎫

84 Round plain ⎬ Mustards.

85 Square ⎭

86 Round Strawberry Dish and Stand, 8 to 10 Inches.

87 Oval ditto   ditto   **8 to 12 Inches.**

88 Platt Menage, 12 Inches high.

89 Water Bottle and Bason, from **2** Pints to **6** Pints each

90 Ice Cellar.

91 Oval ⎫

     ⎬ Bakers, from 6 to 16 Inches.

92 Round ⎭

93 Plain ⎫

     ⎬ Ice Pails, for 1, 2, 3, and 4 Pint Bottles.

94 Fluted ⎭

95 Glass Tray for Ten or Twelve Glasses, 9 to 14 Inches.

96 Double Pail and Ladle.

97 Single   ditto.

98 Oval Water Dish for Dishes of all Sizes.

99 Asparagus Shell.

100 Escollop'd Nappy, from 5 to 16 Inches.

101 Oval Octagon Sallad, from 8 to 13 Inches.

102 Large Furnish'd Castor.

103 Small   ditto.

104 Oil and Vinegar Stand.

105 Grand Platt Menage, 17 Inches high.

106 Grand Platt Menage, 25 Inches high.

107 Small Composite Candlestick, 8 Inches high

108 Dolphin   ditto   10 Inches high.

109 Toilet   ditto $6\frac{1}{2}$ Inches high.

110 Ditto   ditto $6\frac{1}{2}$ Inches high.

111 Ditto   ditto $6\frac{1}{2}$ Inches high.

112 Ornamented   ditto   11 Inches high.

113 Griffin   ditto   10 Inches high.

114 Square Fluted ditto　　10½ Inches high.

115 Corinthian Candlestick, 10　Inches high.

116 Vase Candlestick, 12 Inches high.

117 Large Composite Candlestick, 12½ Inches high.

118 Flatt　　　ditto.

119 Water Ewer, with Round or Oval Bason.

120 Shell Edged Oval Ewer and Bason.

121 Oval Chamber Pot, Four Sizes.

122 Round Chamber Pot, from 1 Pint to 6 Pints.

123 Spitting Pot without Handle.

124 Ditto　　　handled.

125 Oval Shell Edged Shaving Bason, from 9 to 16 Inches.

126 Round Plain ditto, from 9 to 16 Inches.

127 Table Spoon.

128 Sauce Ladle.

129 Tea or Mustard Spoon.

130 Pierced Sugar Spoon.

131 Pierced Fish Trowel.

132 Pierced Fruit Basket and Stand, from 5 to 12 Inches.

133 Ditto　　ditto　　ditto　　ditto another Pattern.

134 Twig Fruit Basket and Stand, from 4 to 12 Inches.

135 Pierced Cover'd Fruit Basket and Stand, from 7 to 11 Inches.

136 Pierced Fruit Basket and Stand, from 5 to 12 Inches.

137 Chesnut Basket and Stand, from 6 to 11 Inches.

138 Ornamented Jarr or Potpourri, from 6 to 14 Inches.

139 Cockle Pot or Potpouri, from 15 to 18 and 22 Inches high.

140 Caper Jarr or Potpourri, from 6 to 12 Inches high.

141 Flower Cup, from 4 to 10 Inches high.

142 Quintal Flower Horn.

143 Ornamented deep Sweet Meat Cup, 3 Inches.

144 Ditto　　shallow　　ditto　　4½ Inches.

No.

145 Confectionary Basket and Stand, 4 Inches.

146 Pot Pourri, 10 Inches high, the Top being inverted makes a Candlestick, as at A.

147 Furnish'd Ink Stand.

148 Wafer Box.

149 Fountain Ink Stand.

150 Sand Box.

151 Common Ink Stand.

152 Cross, with Holy Water Cup, $8\frac{1}{2}$ Inches high.

153 Oval Concave Terrine, from 8 to 14 Inches.

154 Oval New Royal Terrine, from 8 to 14 Inches.

155 Round Concave Terrine and Stand, from 6 to 12 Inches.

156 Handled Covered Bowl and Stand, from $\frac{1}{4}$ to 8 Pints.

157 Oval Concave

158 Ditto Paris or Plain } Dishes, from 6 to 21 Inches; Round Dishes of same Patterns, from 10 to 19 Inches; also Soup Dishes, each Pattern, round or oval, from 10 to 18 Inches.

159 Ditto Bath

160 Oval Concave Covered or Ragou Dish,

161 Round ditto   ditto   ditto   ditto. } From 10 to 14 Inches.

162 Oval Concave Vegetable Dish, from 10 to 12 Inches.

163 Oval New Royal Sallad, from 6 to 14 Inches.

164 Square Plain Covered or Ragou Dish of 12 Inches.

165 Bath   Table Plates, 9 Inches and a Half.

166 Paris or Plain   Soup   ditto,   same Size.

167 New Queen's   Smaller ditto, from 6 to 9 Inches.

168 Concave   N. B. A the Profiles.

169 Concave Sauce Boat and Stand, from 4 to 7 Inches and a Half.

170 Double Concave Sauce Boat and Stand, $8\frac{3}{4}$ Inches.

171 Oval Plain Butter Tub and Stand, from 4 to 6 Inches.

172 Oval Concave Sauce Terrine, Spoon and Stand, from 4 to 7 Inches.

173 Oval Sugar Cup, pierced Spoon and fast Stand; the Sugar Cup $5\frac{1}{2}$ Inches, the Stand 9 Inches.

174 Oval Butter Tub and fast Stand; the Butter Tub $5\frac{3}{4}$ Inches, the Stand $12\frac{1}{2}$ Inches.

No.

175 Oval Radish Dish, 12½ Inches.

176 Mustard, Spoon and fast Stand; the Mustard 2¾ Inches, the Stand 6 Inches Diameter.

177 Double Mustards and Stand; the Stand 7½ Inches.

178 Double Egg Cups and Stand; the Stand 6½ Inches.

179 Ice Pot.

180 Cream Pot covered.

181 Glass Tray, 4¼ Inches Diameter, and 4½ Inches high.

182 Ditto ditto, 4½ Inches ditto, and 4½ Inches ditto.

183 Ditto ditto, 3½ Inches ditto, and 3½ Inches ditto.

184 Bottle Stand pierced, 5 Inches.

185 Ditto ditto plain, ditto.

186 Glass Stand plain, 3¼ Inches.

187 Ditto ditto pierced ditto.

188 Fluted and plain randed Round Ewer and Oval Bason,

189 Oval plain Ewer and Bason,

190 Fluted and Shell Edged Round Ewer and Oval Bason,

191 Oval Shell Edged Ewer and Bason,

Three Sizes to each Pattern.

192 Oval Shell-Edged Covered Ewer and Bason; the Ewer 10 Inches high and Bason 14 Inches long.

193 Water Closet Pot, 12½ Inches Diameter and 14½ Inches high.

194 Stool Pot, from 6 to 14 Inches.

195 Bidet, 17 Inches long.

196 Oval Chamber Pot; Four Sizes.

197 Ditto ditto plain; Two Sizes.

198 Round Bowl for washing or bleeding the Feet in, 14 Inches Diameter.

199 Oval Shaving Bason from 10 to 15 Inches.

200 Round ditto ditto 11 and 12 Inches.

201 Furnished pierced Ink Stand, 8¼ Inches long.

202 Furnished Ink Stand, the Stand 11 Inches.

203 Pot Pourri, or ornamented Vase, from 5 to 11 Inches.

No.

204 Oval ornamented Flower Pot, 11 Inches high.

205 Pot Pourri, or ornamented Vase, from 5 to 11 Inches.

206 Oil and Vinegar Stand, 11 Inches.

207 Spitting Pot, 5 and 6 Inches Diameter.

208 Round Vase Shape Ewer and Bason, of Three Sizes.

209 Covered Water Pot, from 2 to 4 Pints.

210 Oval Fish Dish, from 20 to 30 Inches.

211 Salver or Cheese Stand, from 10 to 17 Inches.

212 Toast Rack.

213 Oval Dish Cover, to fit Dishes, from 10 to 18 Inches.

214 Oval Plain Sallad, ⎫
                    ⎬ from 6 to 14 Inches.
215 Oval Royal Sallad, ⎭

216 Eye Cup.

217 Cafferole, from 4 to 9 Inches.

218 Egg Pan, from 3 to 5 Inches.

219 Sick Pot, 4 and 5 Inches Diameter.

220 Oval Concave Salt.

221 Round plain Salt.

TEA WARE.

No.

1 Plain Square Tea Pot.

2 Fluted Square Tea Pot.

3 Round Plain ditto.

4 Round Fluted ditto.

5 Plain Coffee Pot }
6 Fluted ditto. } with Spouts.

7 Plain Coffee Pot }
8 Fluted ditto. } with Snips.

9 Fluted Cannister.

10 Square ditto.

11 Plain ditto.

12 Fluted Milk Pot.

13 Plain ditto.

14 Plain Slop Bowl.

15 Fluted ditto.

16 Plain Milk Ewer.

17 Fluted ditto.

18 Square pierced Tea or Coffee Tray, from 10 to 19 Inches.

19 Fluted handled Sugar Cup.

20 Plain ditto ditto.

21 Fluted Sugar Cup.

22 Plain ditto.

23 Pierced ditto.

24 Ditto ditto

No.

25 Square Chocolate

26 Common Chocolate } A; the Saucer for ditto.

27 Handled Tea Cup

28 Tea Cup not handled

29 Fluted Square Chocolate

30 Ditto   common ditto. } A; the Saucer for ditto.

31 Ditto   handled Tea Cup

32 Ditto   not handled ditto.

33 Chocolate Stand, from 6 to 8 Inches.

34 Ditto   ditto.

35 Ditto   ditto.

36 Ditto   ditto.

37 Ditto   ditto.

38 Ditto   ditto.

39 Ditto   ditto.

40 Ditto   ditto.

41 Ditto $8\frac{1}{2}$ Inches.

42 Ditto   from 6 to 8 Inches.

43 Ditto   ditto.

44 Ditto $8\frac{1}{2}$ Inches Diameter.

45 Sugar Cup.

46 Ditto.

47 Ditto.

48 Ditto.

Leeds Pottery

Leeds Pottery

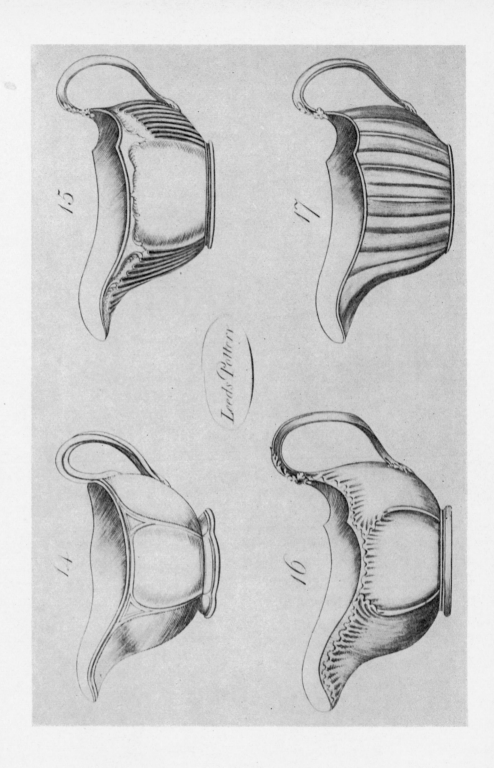

Leeds Pottery

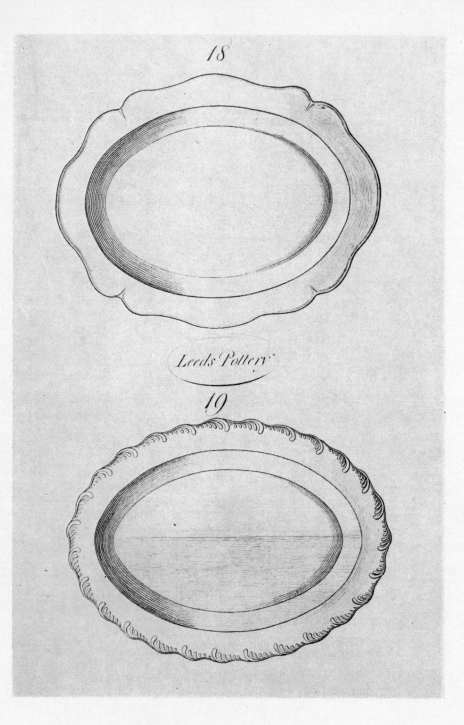

18

Leeds Pottery

19

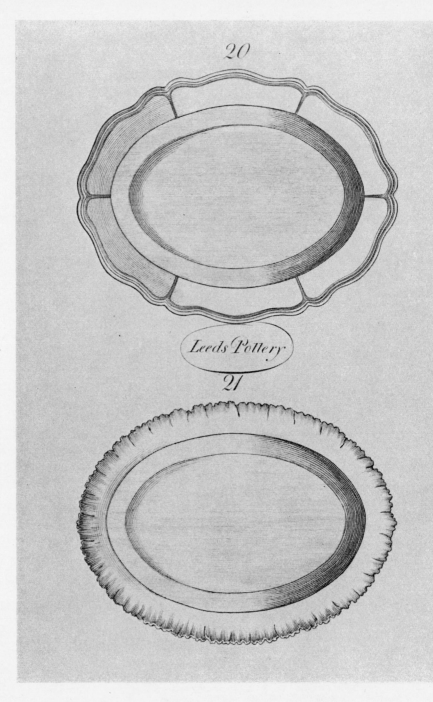

20

Leeds Pottery

21

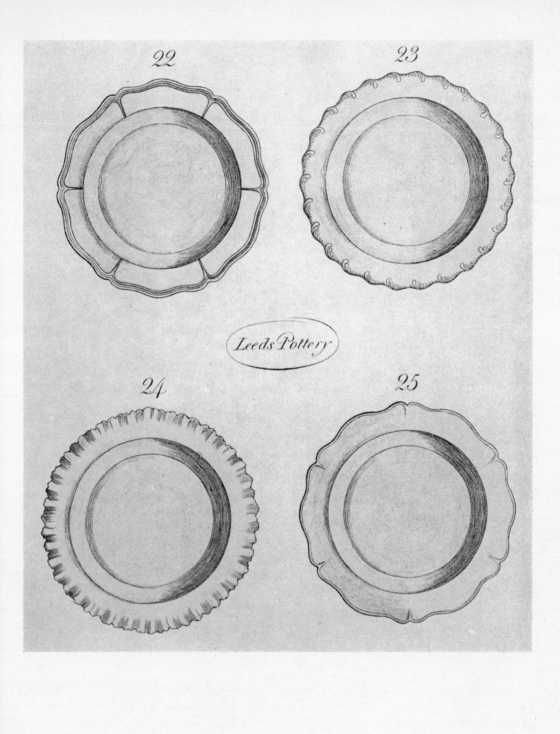

22   23

Leeds Pottery

24   25

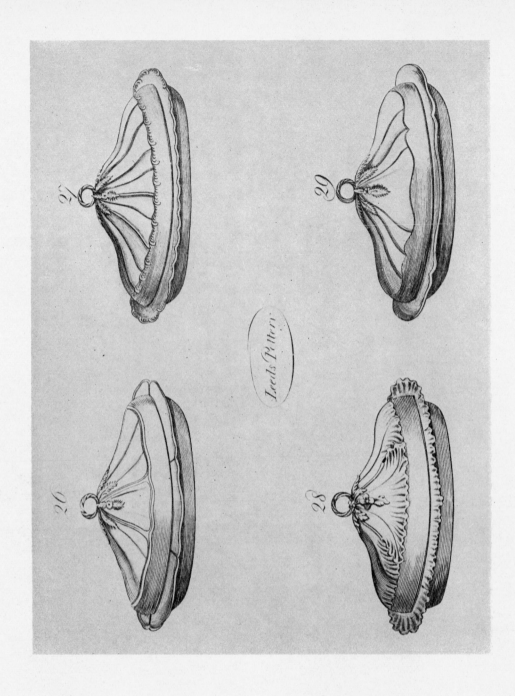

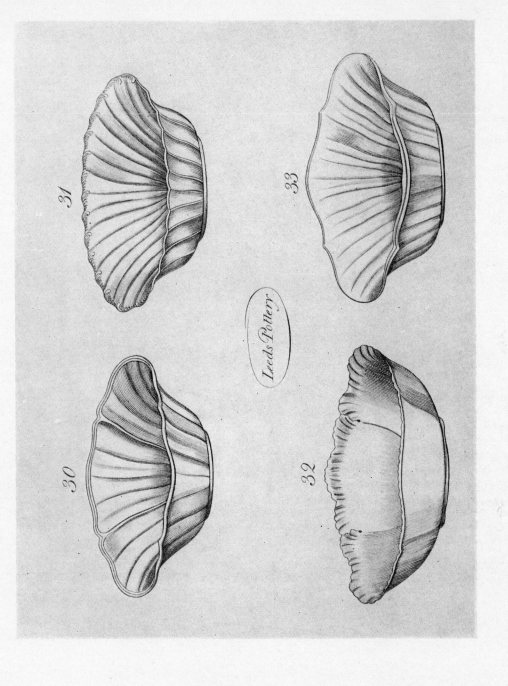

31

33

Leeds Pottery

30

32

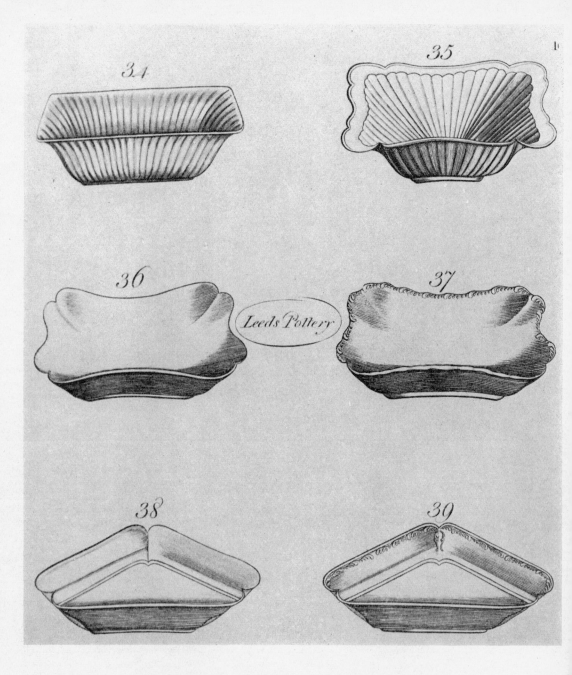

34

35

36

Leeds Pottery

37

38

39

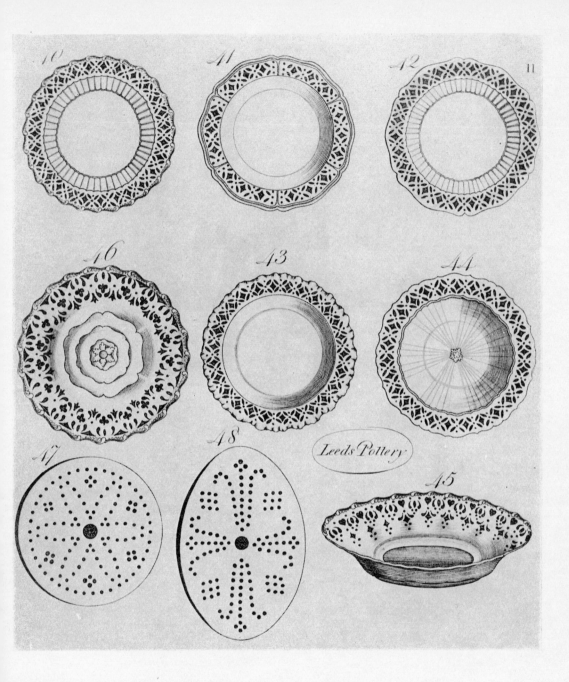

Leeds Pottery

49   50

51   52

53   54

Leeds Pottery

55 56 57 13

Leeds Pottery

58 59

60   61

Leeds Pottery

62

63

64 65

Leeds Pottery

66 67

Leeds Pottery

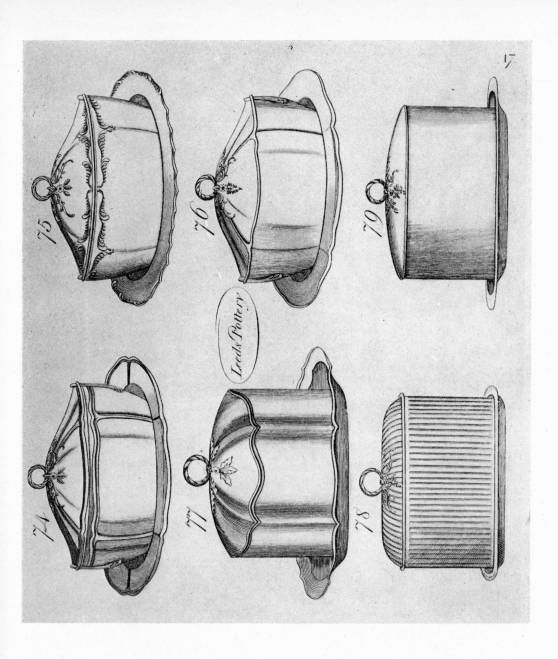

75

76

79

Leeds Pottery

74

77

78

Leeds Pottery

Leeds Pottery

Leeds Pottery

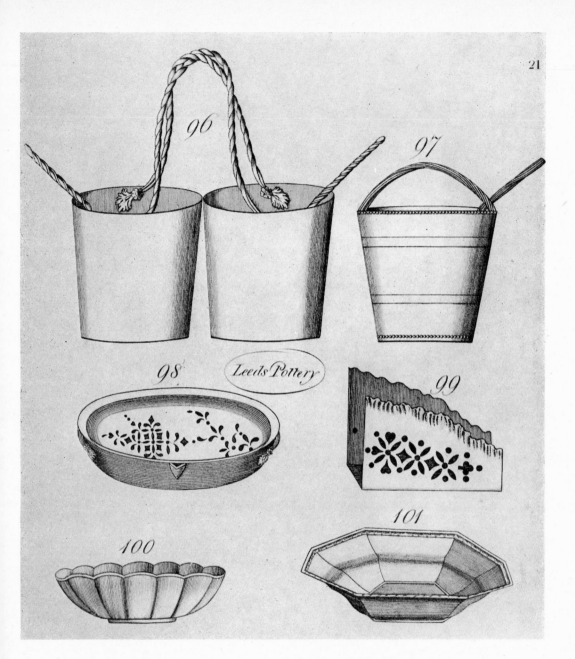

96

97

98

Leeds Pottery

99

100

101

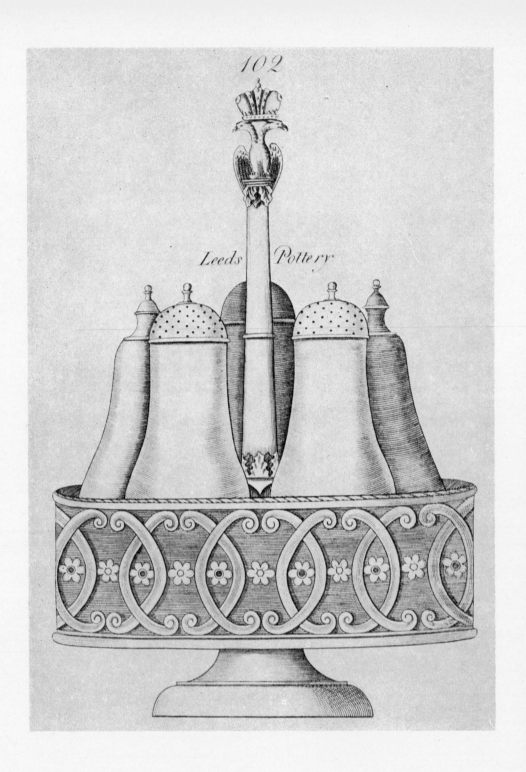

103

Leeds Pottery

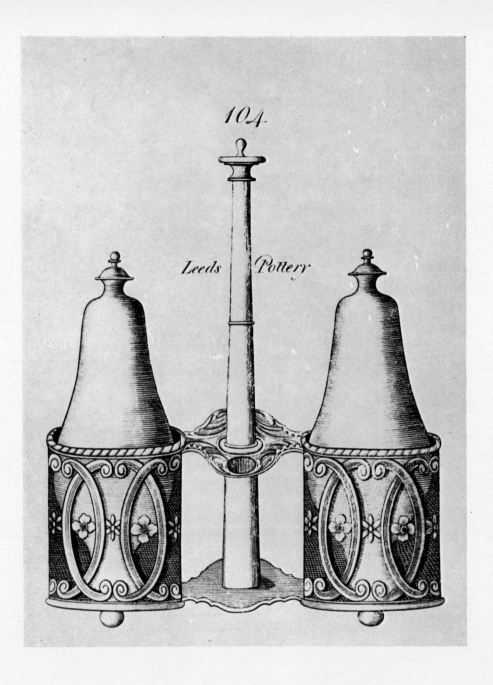

104.

Leeds Pottery

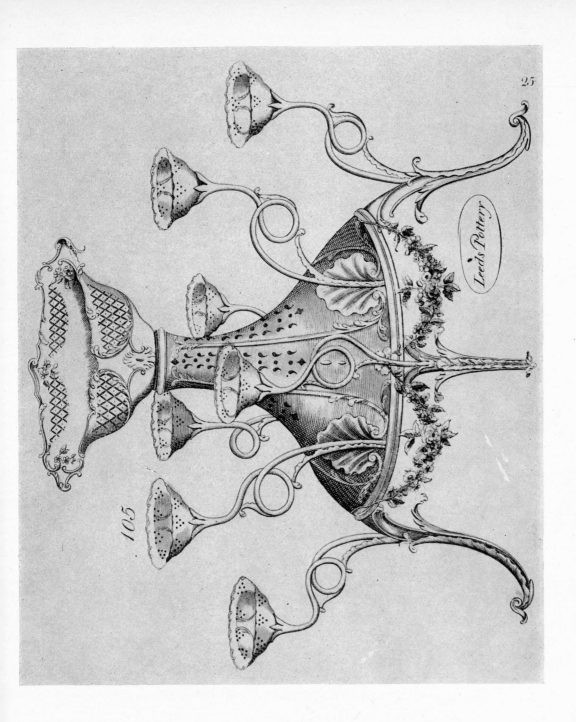

Leeds Pottery

105

106

Leeds Pottery

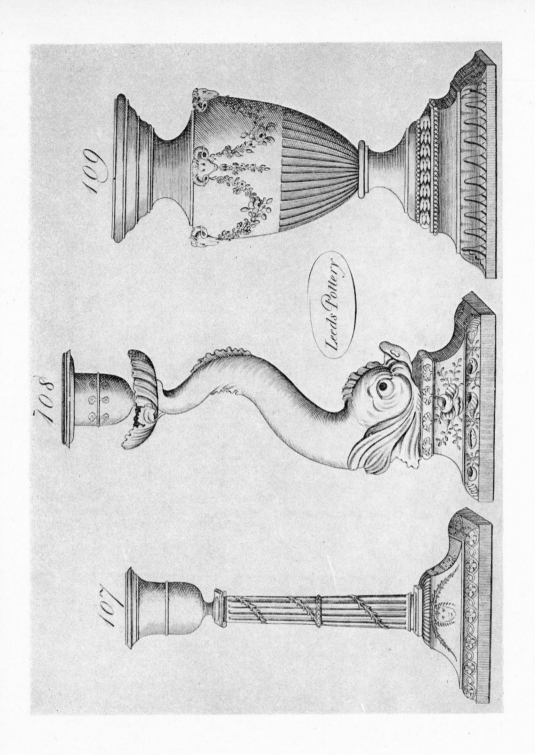

109

108

107

Leeds Pottery

117

116

115

118

Leeds Pottery

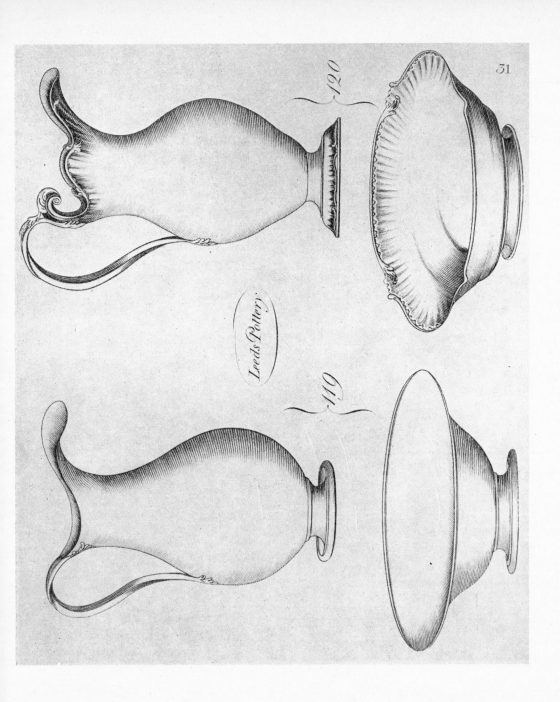

120

119

Leeds Pottery.

121

122

123

124

Leeds Pottery

125

126

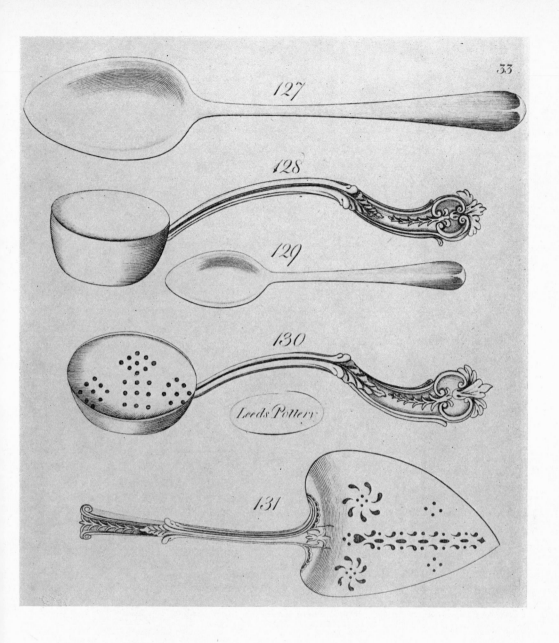

127

128

129

130

Leeds Pottery

131

132

133

34

134

135

Leeds Pottery

136

137

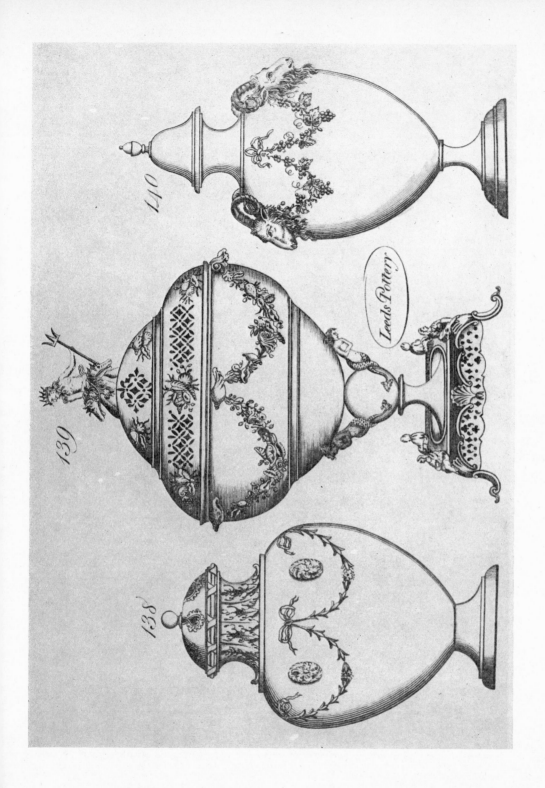

140

139

138

Leeds Pottery

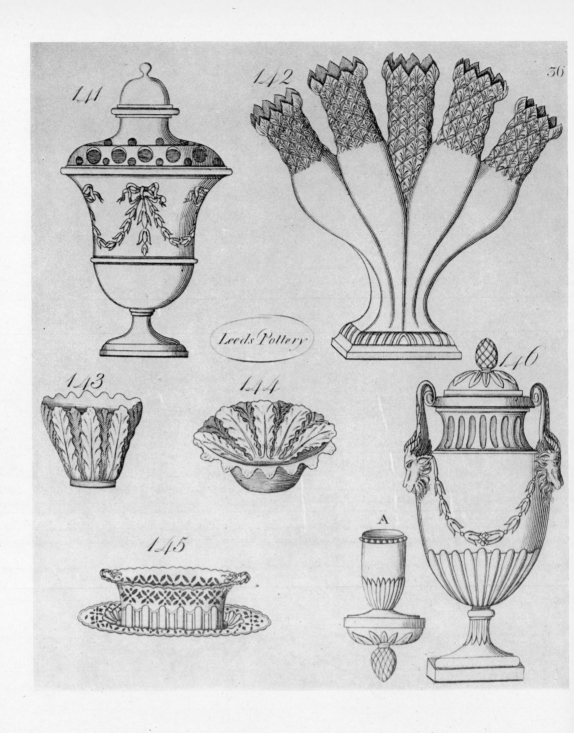

141   142

Leeds Pottery

143   144   146

145   A

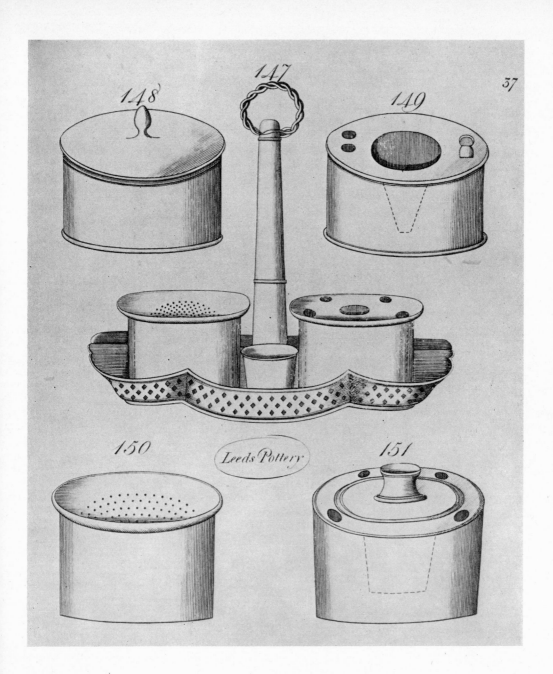

147

148

149

150

Leeds Pottery

151

152

INRI

Leeds Pottery

Nº 153

154

Leeds Pottery

155

156

Leeds Pottery

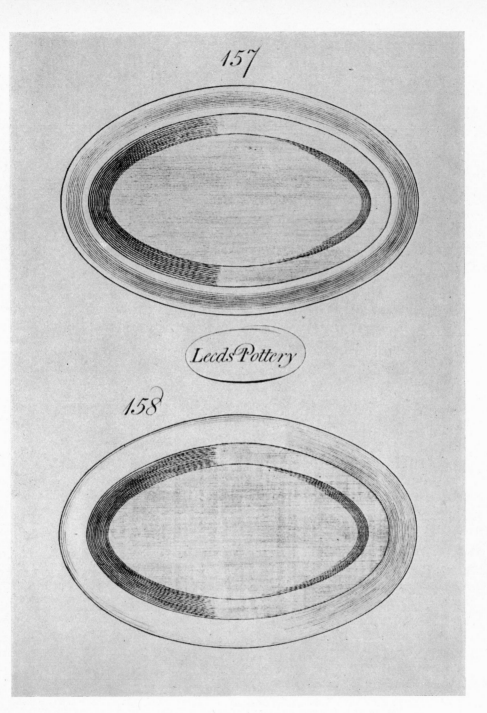

157

Leeds Pottery

158

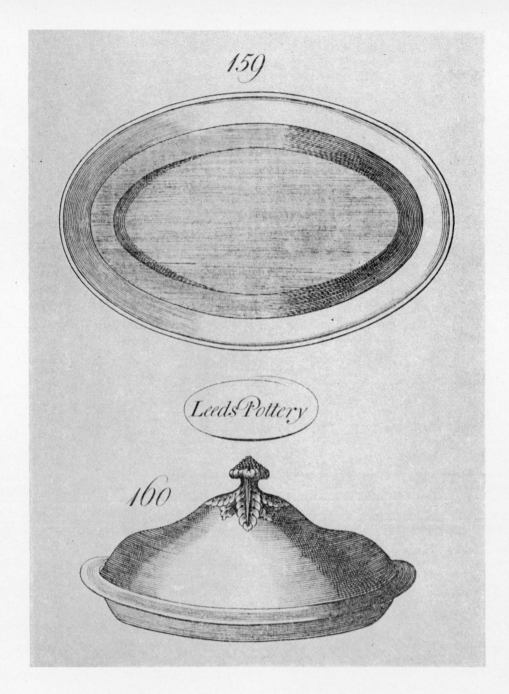

159

Leeds Pottery

160

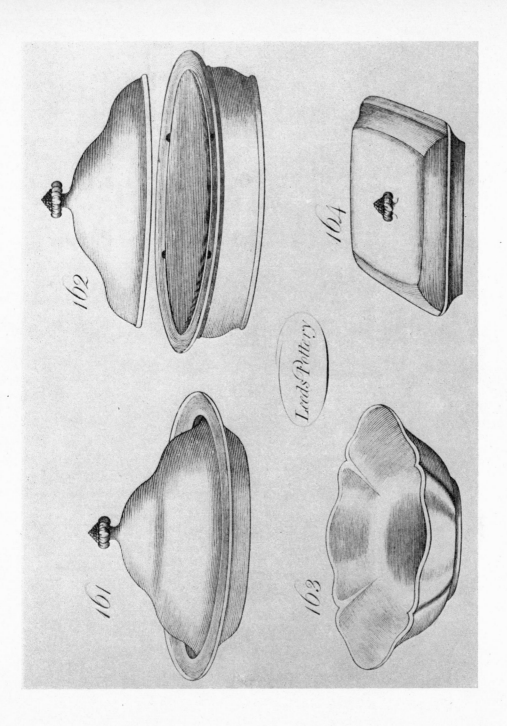

162

164

Leeds Pottery

161

163

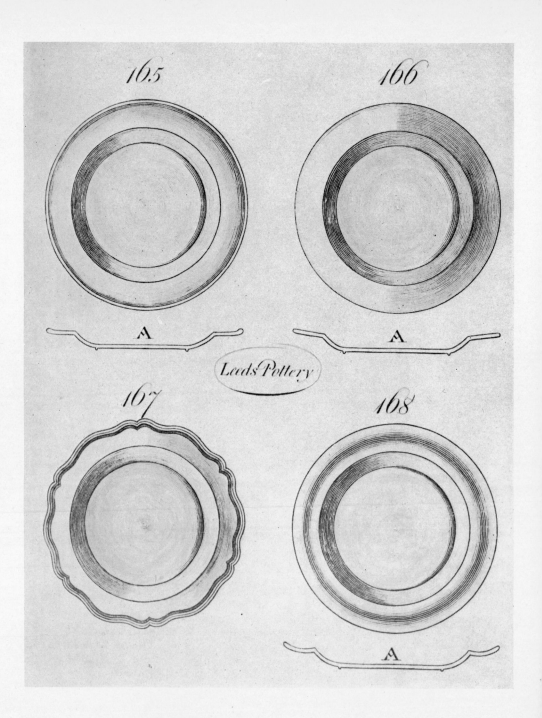

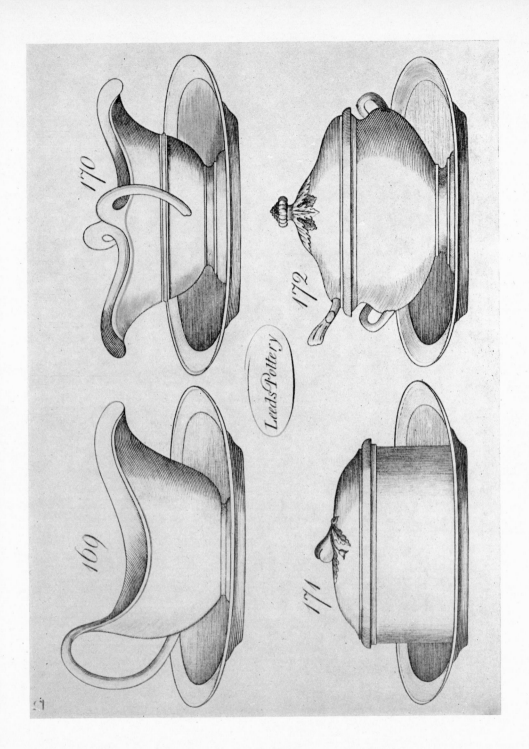

Leeds Pottery

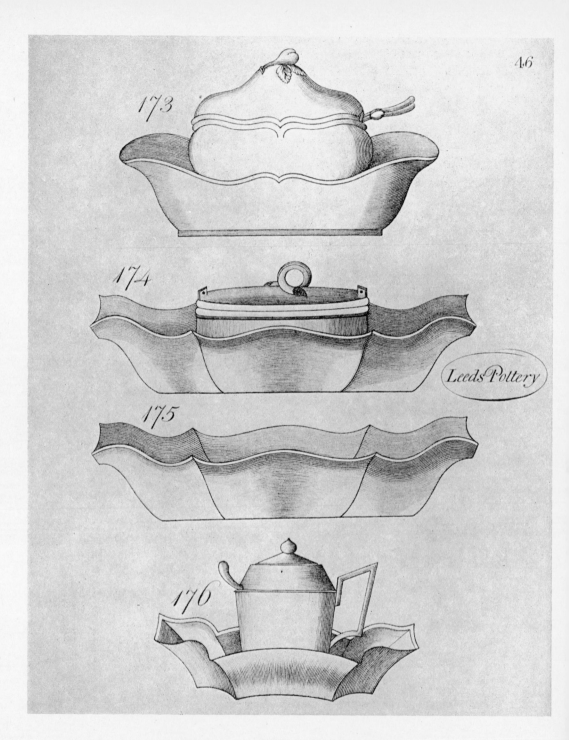

173

174

Leeds Pottery

175

176

177

178

Leeds Pottery

179

180

181   182   183

184

185

186   187

Leeds Pottery

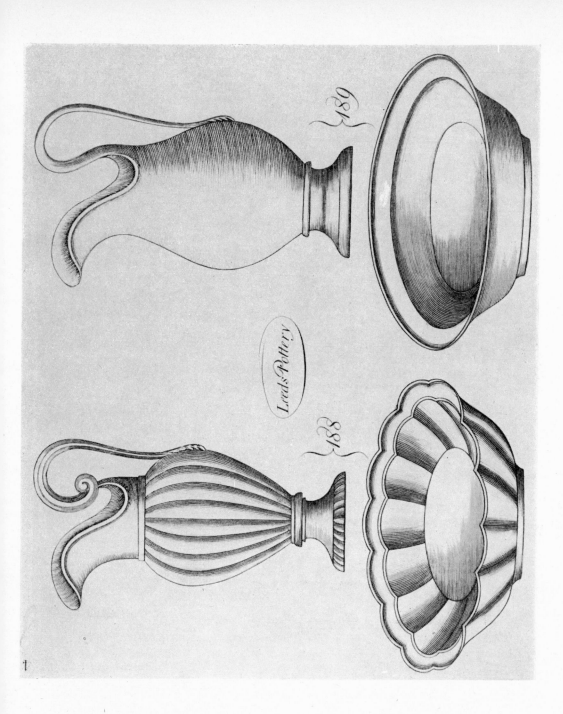

189

188

Leeds Pottery

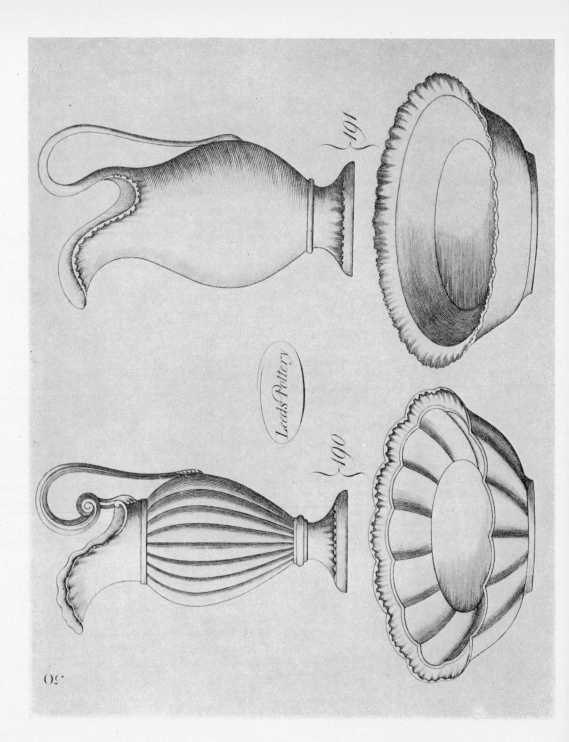

Leeds Pottery

50

Leeds Pottery

192

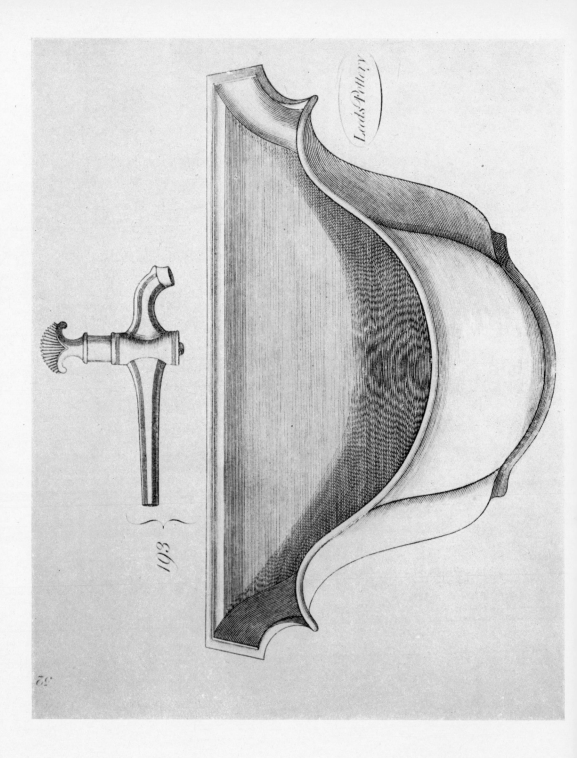

194

Leeds Pottery

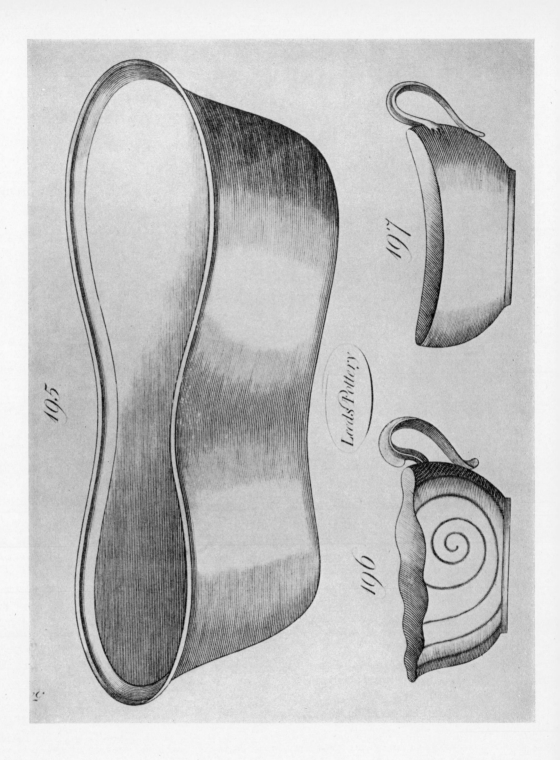

195

197

Leeds Pottery

196

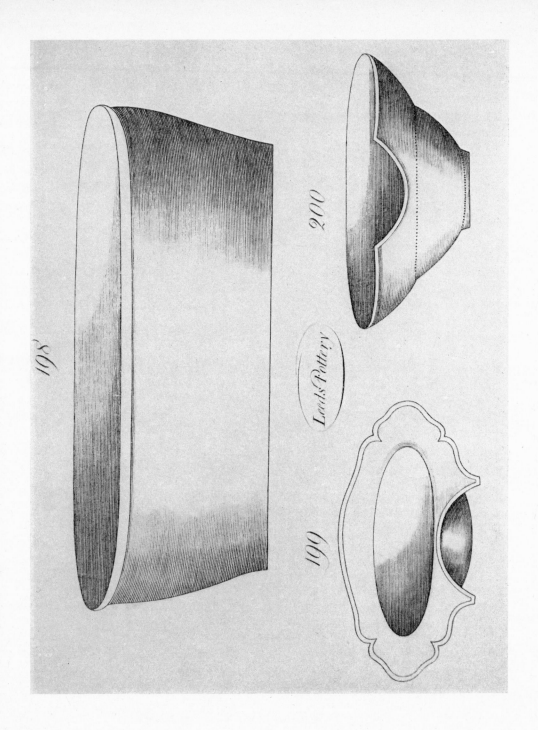

198

200

Leeds Pottery

199

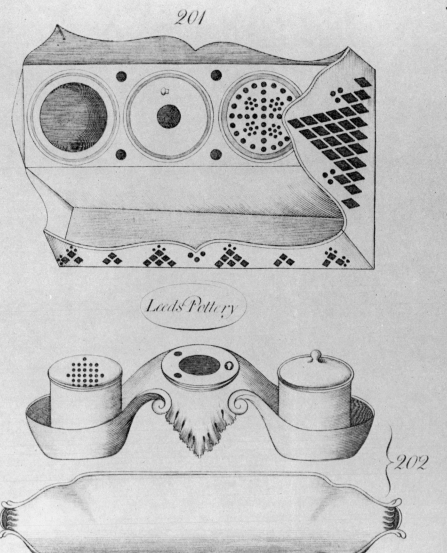

201

Leeds Pottery

202

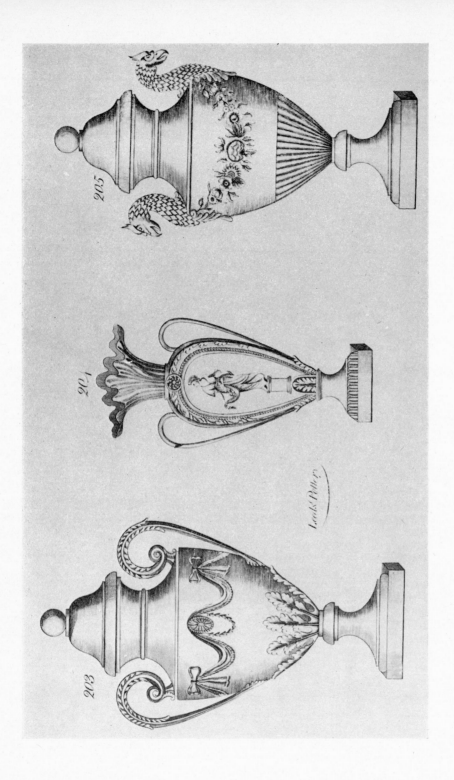

Leeds Pottery.

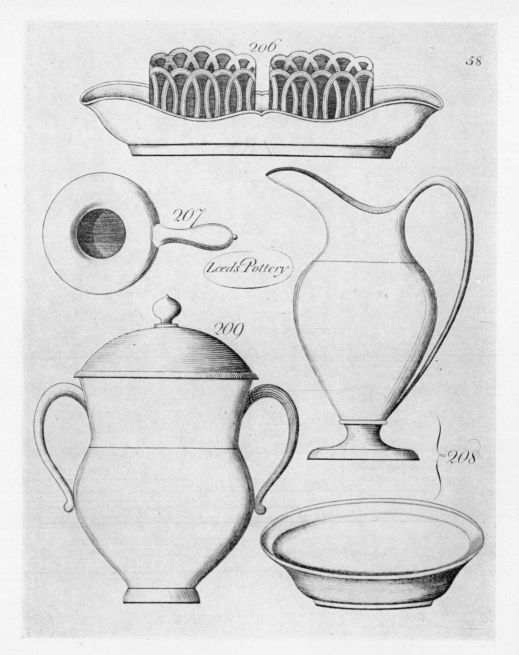

206

207

Leeds Pottery

209

208

210

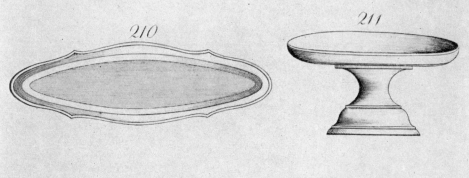

211

212

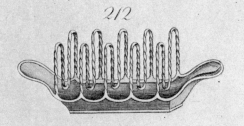

213

Leeds Pottery

214

215

216

217

218

219

Leeds Pottery

220

221

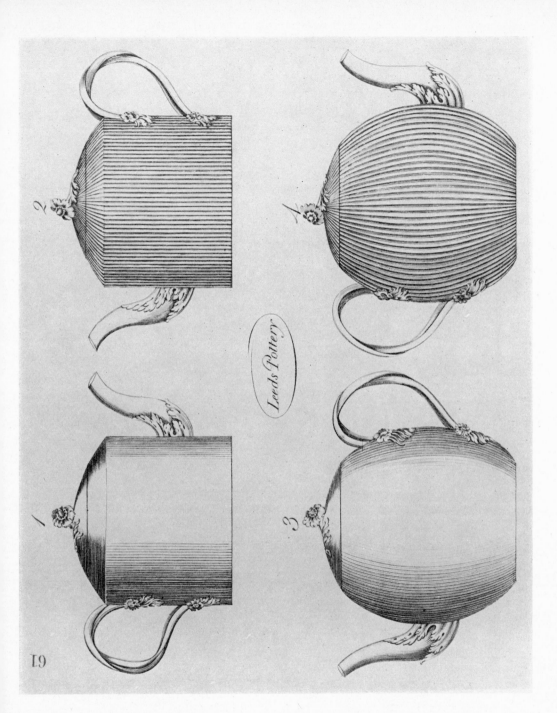

Leeds Pottery

61

Leeds Pottery

Leeds Pottery

Leeds Pottery

Leeds Pottery

25

26

Leeds Pottery

27

28

A

29   30   67

Leeds Pottery

31   32

A

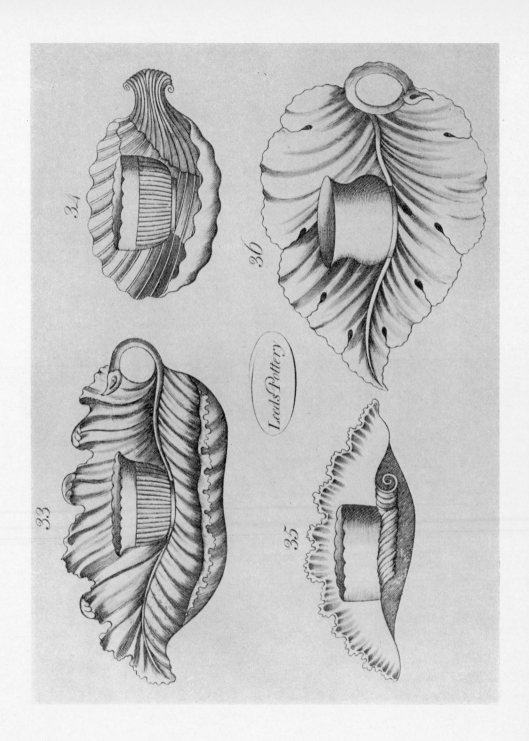

34

36

33

35

Leeds Pottery

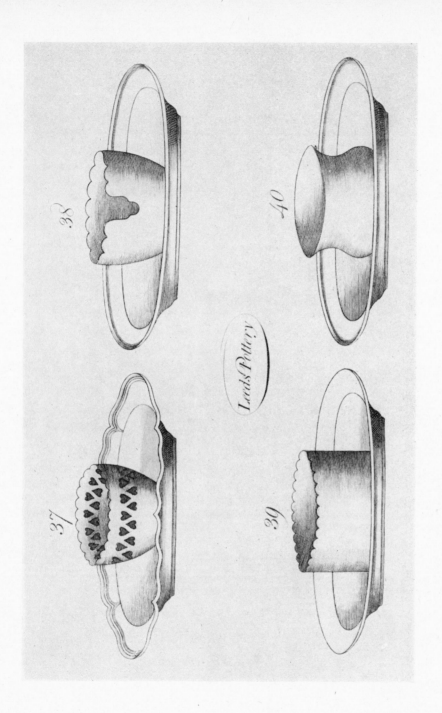

37

38

39

40

Leeds Pottery

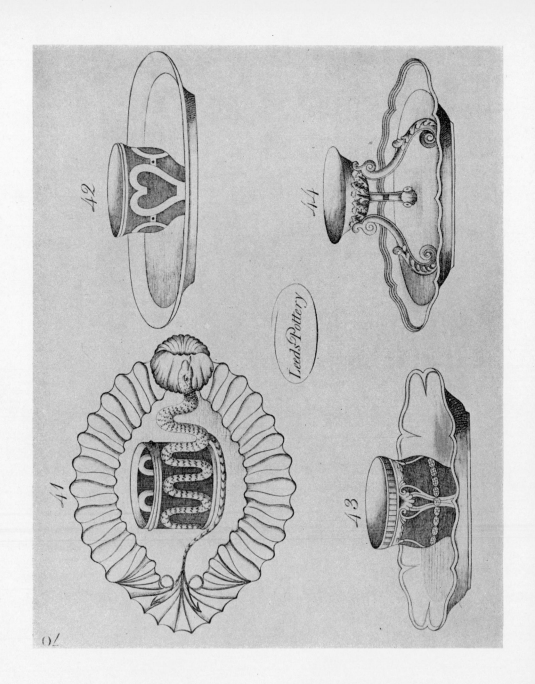

42

44

41

43

Leeds Pottery

70

45

46

Leeds Pottery

47

48

The Marks

MUCH OF THE DIFFICULTY of identifying Leeds Pottery is due to the scarcity of marked pieces. At first only those pieces illustrated in the Leeds Pattern Books were regularly marked, but other Yorkshire creamware factories, in order to supplement their stocks or make up their orders, bought from the Leeds Pottery, and instructions are given in the Leeds order books that all such orders should be marked. For instance, the entry 'Ordered from Swinton, to be marked' occurs a number of times in the account books and a similar entry is also made for Hull. In addition certain private orders include the request for the wares to be marked. An instance of this is to be found in *Drawing Book No.* 2 at the Victoria and Albert Museum and reads 'Il Tutto Marcato Hartlei Greens C', which is translated by the Pottery 'the whole marked underneath, Hartley Greens & Co., Leeds Pottery'. Subsequently 'Hartley Greens & Co.' was struck out, leaving the more usual mark 'Leeds Pottery'. In the course of time the practice of marking the ware became more usual, and after 1790 quite a large proportion of pearlware, particularly the figures; blackware and blue-printed ware was marked, though the marked creamware, except for the figures, usually corresponded with the illustrated pieces in the Pattern Books as before. For the most part the Leeds factory marks which are illustrated at the end of this chapter (pages 144 and 145) consisted of the words LEEDS POTTERY accompanied by various notation marks, impressed underneath the ware. The earliest known mark consists of the words LEEDS ∗ POTTERY separated by an asterisk (Fig. 5, 1, page 144) and is impressed under a deep cream-coloured shell sweetmeat dish which was made before 1775 (Plate 12a). There is little difference between this mark and those immediately succeeding it except as to the type used. It will be seen that the lower part of the curve of the D, P and R are oblique and that the type is somewhat taller than that used for the slightly later marks. Fig. 5: 2 to 5, page 144, occur on some of the Leeds wares made between 1775 and 1790. The asterisk is sometimes placed at the end instead of in the middle as in Fig. 5, 4, page 144, and is sometimes replaced by either a hyphen or a full stop. Whether these signs had any significance is not known. A large impressed numeral sometimes occurs close to the factory mark.

Before about 1790 the letters comprising the marks were irregularly placed. In Fig. 5: 15, page 144, which occurs on a piece of blue-printed ware (Plate 48, i), a small 's' has been used, and in one known instance several of the letters are in the wrong order, making it quite clear that the type was fitted into a holder, the impression of the edge of which is sometimes visible. A stoneware die was made for most marks used after about 1790, with the result that the impression became regular. One of these stoneware dies bearing the mark (Fig. 5: 16, page 144) is at the Harrogate Museum and was probably made soon after 1800. Dies were presumably also made for Fig. 5: 9, 11, 12, 16, 17, 18 and 21, page 144. Fig. 5: 9, 11 and 12, page 144, are also to be found on some creamware of comparatively recent manufacture. In these the letters are more square, regular and closely arranged than in the earlier marks. Their usual measurement taken from the tip of the L to the extreme tip of the Y is $\frac{7}{8}$ in. to $\frac{5}{16}$ in., although Fig. 5: 11, page 144, is usually larger, whereas the earlier marks all seem to have been more than an inch long and usually range between $1\frac{1}{8}$ in. and $1\frac{1}{2}$ in. Different types were used for Fig. 5: 6, 8, 11 and 12, page 144. Fig. 5: 8, page 144, which is in oblique type, occurs on the Dutch painted teapot on Plate 31a. Fig. 5: 7, page 144, is the mark used for most of the Leeds Pottery pearlware figures, which are sometimes impressed twice. The significance of the double marks, Fig. 5: 13, 14 and 15, page 144, in which the second stamp is impressed across the first, forming a cross, is uncertain, especially in view of the fact that in marked services both the cross mark and the single mark occur in seemingly one and the same service (Plate 48). The Hartley Greens & Co. marks, Fig. 5: 16, 17, 18, 19 and 21, page 144, were introduced soon after 1800. The letters LP (Fig. 5: 20, page 144), are occasionally to be found impressed under the ware, especially transfer-printed ware, but the mark is rare (Plate 35a). The letters LP also occur painted on the saddle-cloth of a Leeds figure of a horse in the Yorkshire Museum. Fig. 6: 30, page 145, is incised under the 'vase candlestick' illustrated on Plate 23. Fig. 6: 22, 22a and 23, page 145, are transfer-printed and are sometimes to be found on the Leeds transfer-printed ware as part of the print (Plates 34a, 35b, 36a, b). Fig. 6: 27 and 35, page 145, are late marks of the factory (Fig. 6: 27, page 145, being that of Richard Britton & Sons, 1872–8). Fig. 6: 35, page 145, was used during the Warburton period, 1853–61. Fig. 5: 29, page 144, is a fake and occurs incised on a creamware plaque fitted into the base of a Wedgwood coffee-pot at the Leeds City Art Gallery. No such mark was used by the Leeds Pottery. The mark HM (Fig. 6: 39, page 145) is impressed under the covers of some creamware of excellent quality which is invariably enamelled with floral sprays in

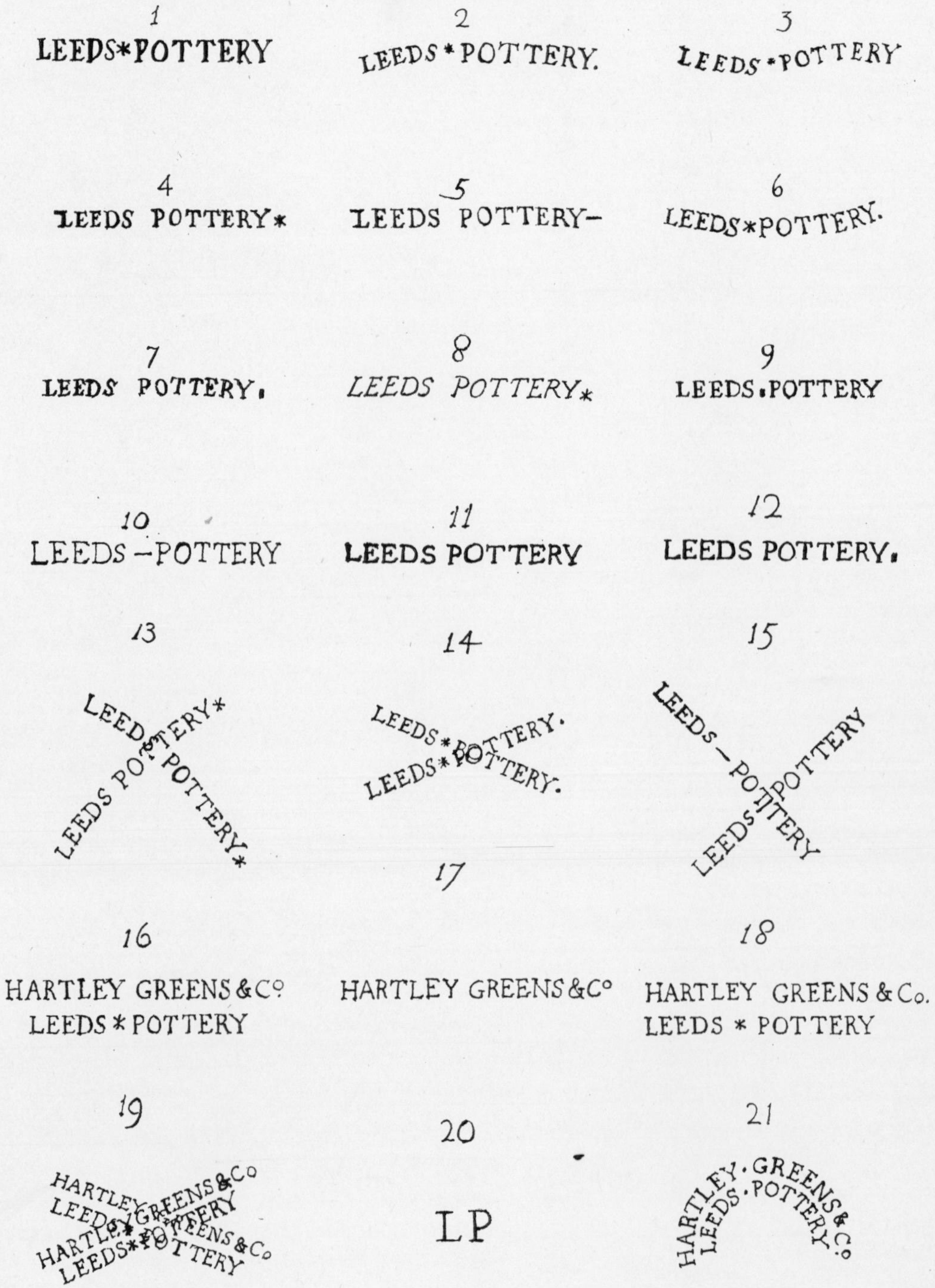

1

LEEDS*POTTERY

2

LEEDS*POTTERY.

3

LEEDS*POTTERY

4

LEEDS POTTERY*

5

LEEDS POTTERY—

6

LEEDS*POTTERY.

7

LEEDS POTTERY.

8

LEEDS POTTERY

9

LEEDS.POTTERY

10

LEEDS—POTTERY

11

LEEDS POTTERY

12

LEEDS POTTERY.

13

LEEDS POTTERY*
LEEDS POTTERY*

14

LEEDS*POTTERY.
LEEDS*POTTERY.

15

LEEDS—POTTERY
LEEDS POTTERY

16

HARTLEY GREENS & Cº
LEEDS*POTTERY

17

HARTLEY GREENS & Cº

18

HARTLEY GREENS & Co.
LEEDS*POTTERY

19

HARTLEY GREENS & Cº
LEEDS POTTERY
HARTLEY GREENS & Co
LEEDS*POTTERY

20

LP

21

HARTLEY.GREENS & Cº
LEEDS.POTTERY

Fig. 5

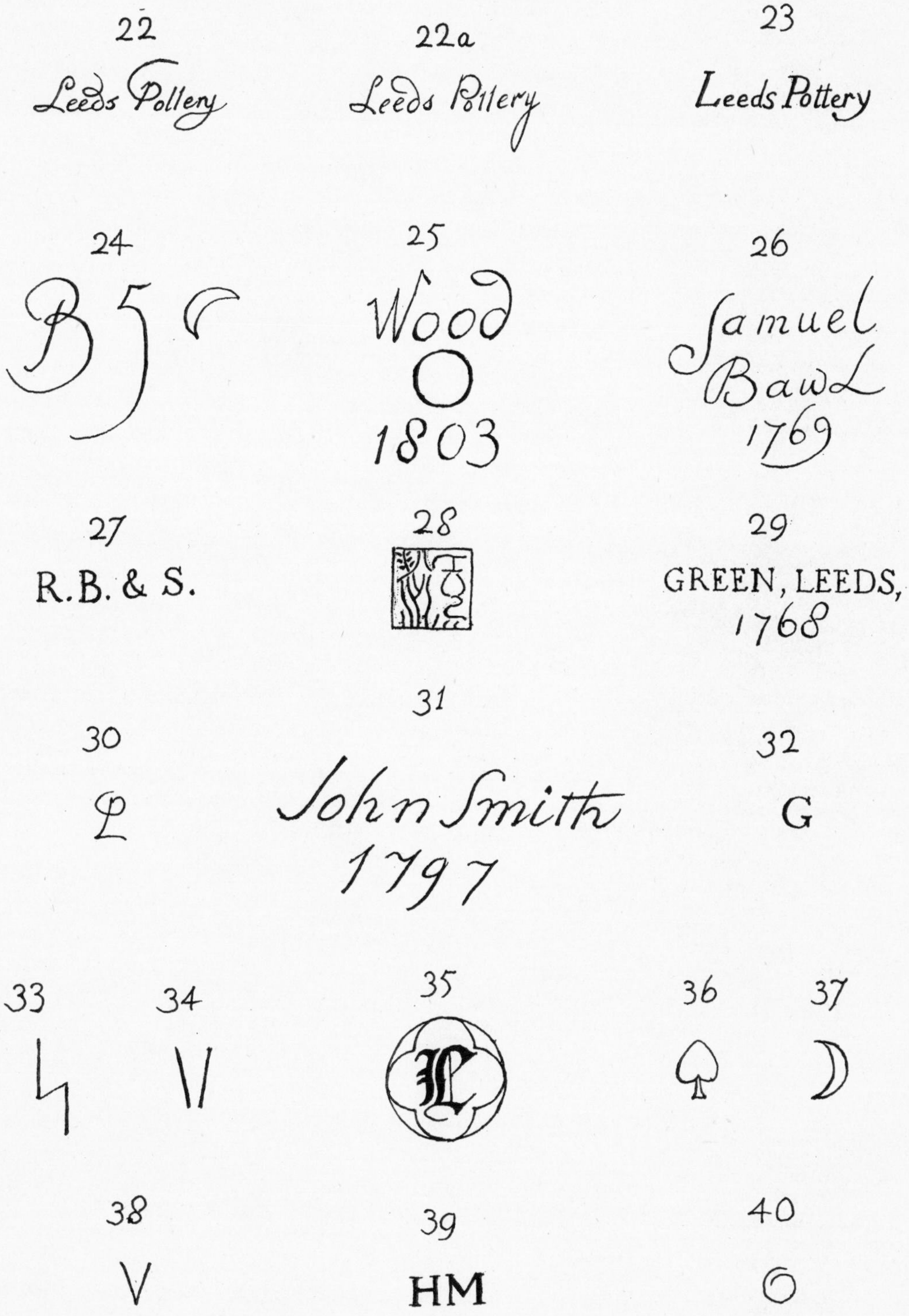

22
Leeds Pottery

22a
Leeds Pottery

23
Leeds Pottery

24
B J C

25
Wood
O
1803

26
Samuel
Bawl
1769

27
R. B. & S.

28

29
GREEN, LEEDS,
1768

30
P

31
John Smith
1797

32
G

33
4

34
V

35

36
♠

37
)

38
V

39
HM

40
Ꝋ

Fig. 6

purplish crimson and may be the product of the Holbeck Moor factory, a close neighbour of the Leeds Pottery, but as precisely the same painting occurs on Leeds creamware (Plate 30a, iii) and the ware is in other ways similar, it may be the mark of one of the Leeds potters or have some other meaning. Incised marks of Leeds potters are Fig. 6: 24, 25, 26, 32, 33, 34, 36, 37 and 40, page 145. Of these Fig. 6: 24 is incised (the crescent impressed) under a block-mould of a sauce boat, from the Leeds Pottery; Fig. 6: 25, is incised under a puzzle-jug (Plate 44a, ii) and Fig. 5: 26 is incised under the 'John Wilkes' snuff-box (Plate 12b). Fig. 6: 38, page 145, painted in underglaze blue is sometimes to be found under the so-called Batavian ware and is a painter's mark. Fig. 6: 31, page 145, is incised under a figure of a flute-player at the Yorkshire Museum (Plate 38a). Since this figure is clearly by the same hand as most, if not all, of the Leeds figures, it is evident that John Smith was the principal Leeds figure modeller, and one is tempted to conjecture whether this modeller and John Smith of the Rothwell Pottery are one and the same person (page 169). Red stoneware made at the Leeds Pottery was sometimes stamped underneath with an imitation seal mark (Fig. 6: 28, page 145) (Plate 2).

CHAPTER TEN

Moulded Details

MUCH HELP IN IDENTIFYING the origins of wares can often be gained from a knowledge of the various moulded details used by the different factories. Some patterns were used by a number of factories, while others seem to have been peculiar to one only. The following notes are the result of a careful study over a period of many years of the moulded details found on the wares of all the known English earthenware factories. The drawings to which they refer will be found on pages 148, 150, 152–3 and are made from actual pieces of Leeds creamware, though it must be pointed out that the Leeds Pottery produced many other patterns; but the illustrations show those of most frequent occurrence and are therefore the most typical of the factory.

FIGURE 7, HANDLES

Fig. 7: 1, page 148. The crabstock handle (Plates 4, 10b, 16a) was used in conjunction with the crabstock spout (Fig. 8: 1, page 150) by many potteries, including the Leeds Pottery, approximately between 1745 and 1770, and occurs on teapots and punch-pots of creamware, including various forms of colour-glazed ware; red stoneware, glazed black earthenware, and saltglaze.

Fig. 7: 2, page 148. The flat loop handle (Plate 3) was made at a number of potteries in Staffordshire, at Derby, and at Leeds between about 1740 and 1770. It was used for jugs, mugs, and coffee-pots, of saltglaze, creamware, glazed black earthenware, solid agate ware, and red stoneware (Plate 3).

Fig. 7: 2a, page 148, shows a variation of the pinched end to this handle.

Fig. 7: 3, page 148. The indented loop handle (Plates 30b, 34a) was used by the Leeds Pottery as well as by other factories, such as Liverpool, Wedgwood, and Turner. It also occurs very frequently on a large group of teapots decorated with transfer-prints engraved by William Greatbatch (page 39). The section of this handle sometimes varies slightly according to its provenance.

Fig. 7: 4, page 148. The double reeded strap handle (Plate 17a) occurs on some Leeds creamware made before 1775, usually in conjunction with the spout, Fig. 8: 3, page 150. It may also have been used at Derby.

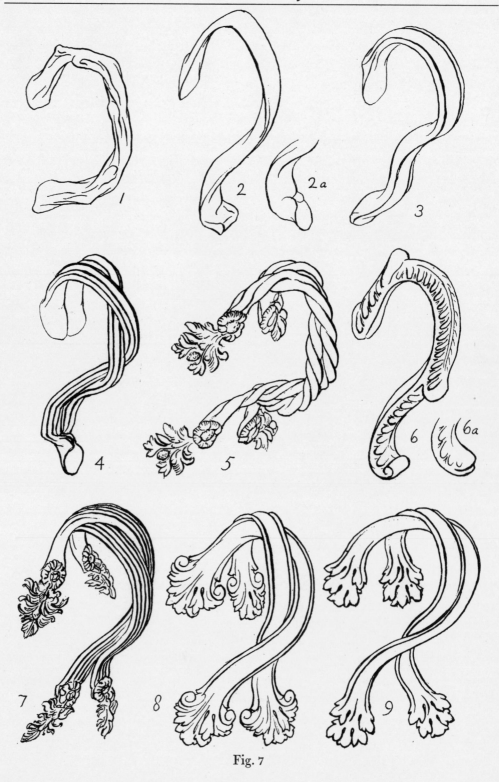

Fig. 7

Fig. 7: 5, page 148. The double rope or twisted handle (Plates 13a, ii; 16b) is one of the most characteristic of the early Leeds creamware handles. It may, however, also have been used at the Melbourne Pottery in Derbyshire, but with different terminals.

Fig. 7: 6, page 148. This type of scroll handle which was used on some Leeds creamware before 1775 was no doubt derived from a silver model. It closely resembles a Wedgwood handle, from which it differs in the direction of the ornament in the first (top) section, the curl at the base, and the small nick between each loop of the pattern (*English Cream-coloured Earthenware*, page 75, Fig. 3).

Fig. 7: 7, page 148. The double reeded handle with applied terminals (Plate 26a, etc.) was used extensively by the Leeds Pottery after about 1775. Although the double reeded handle was made by a number of potteries, it varied considerably in the number and form of the reeds or flutings and particularly in regard to the applied terminals, but the precise pattern shown in the drawing Fig. 7: 7, page 148, does not appear to have been used by any factory other than the Leeds Pottery.

Fig. 7: 8, 9, page 148. These two handles (Plate 36a, b) denote a Leeds origin, as they do not appear to have been used by any other factory. They seem to have been first used soon after 1780, and appear on many of the illustrations in the Pattern Book.

FIGURE 8, SPOUTS

Fig. 8: 1, page 150. The crabstock spout (Plates 4, 10b, 16a) was used by a number of factories including the Leeds Pottery for teapots and punch-pots of saltglaze, red stoneware, black earthenware, and creamware, including colour-glazed ware. It seems to have been introduced about 1745 and was discontinued about 1770. It was used in conjuction with the crabstock handle (Fig. 7: 1, page 148).

Fig. 8: 2, page 150. This spout (Plate 16b, i) and several slight variations of it (Plate 10a) were made by the Leeds Pottery. One of these which can be seen on the colour plate facing page 22, may have been used at Derby as well. A later Leeds variation is shown on Plates 10a and 36a, b.

Fig. 8: 3, page 150. This spout was normally used in conjunction with the handle, Fig. 7: 4, page 148, and has so far only been found on Leeds creamware of an early date (Plate 17a), and in one known instance on Cauliflower ware.

Fig. 8: 4, 5, page 150. Spouts with acanthus and other foliate forms at the base (Plate 26a, ii) were used by the Leeds Pottery for both the early and later creamware, but variations of these were used by other factories. Fig. 8: 4, 5, page 150, are the usual Leeds versions.

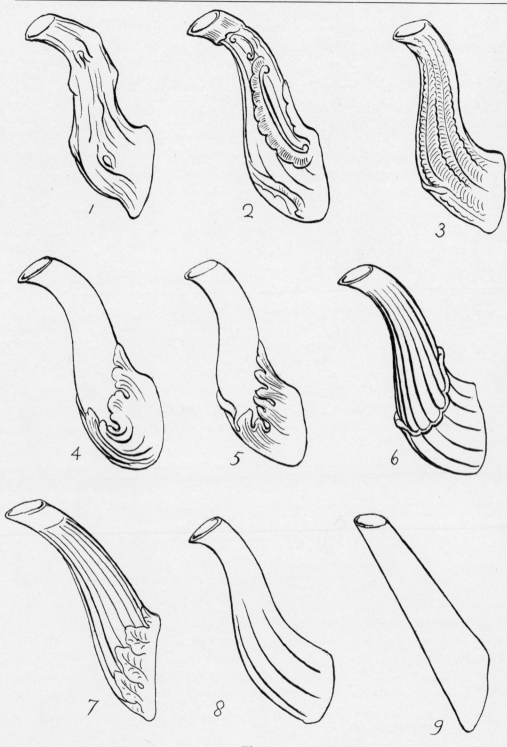

Fig. 8

Fig. 8: 6, page 150. This spout (Plate 26a, i; 27b, ii) appears to be peculiar to the Leeds Pottery and was frequently used for teapots of about 1780.

Fig. 8: 7, page 150. This spout (Plate 26b) was used at Leeds as well as by other factories.

Fig. 8: 8, page 150. This is the Leeds Pattern of the 'shell' spout (Plate 32a) and differs slightly from the Wedgwood version.

Fig. 8: 9, page 150. The straight spout, together with the variation shown on Plate 13a, ii, occurs on creamware of early Leeds manufacture, but it was made by other factories in both red and black stoneware.

FIGURE 9, FLOWER KNOBS

Fig. 9: 1, 1*a*, 1*b*, page 152. The same flower (Plates 26b, ii; 30b, i, ii) is shown on each of these knobs, but the terminal at the base of the flower differs. All three were used at the Leeds Pottery, but Fig. 9: 1, page 152 also occurs on a large group of teapots decorated with transfer-prints of the 'Prodigal Son' and other subjects engraved by William Greatbatch (page 39), and it is probable that many of these were not made at Leeds, but by some other factory, possibly by Greatbatch himself.

Fig. 9: 2, 2*a*, 3, 3*a*, 6, 7, page 152. All these varieties of the convolvulus knob (Plates 13a, ii; 16b, i, ii; 19) though often combined with different terminals, were produced by the Leeds Pottery. Fig. 9: 3, 3*a*, page 152, is particularly indicative of a Leeds origin, but convolvulus knobs closely similar to Fig. 9: 2, 2*a*, page 152, but without terminals, were made in France.

Fig. 9: 4, 4*a*, 4*b*, 4*c*, 5, page 152. These are the flower knobs generally used by the Leeds Pottery after about 1775 and do not appear to have been used elsewhere (Plates 7; 11; 26a, 7, ii; 27a, i, ii, etc.).

FIGURE 10, TERMINALS

Fig. 10: 1, 2, 7, 8, page 153. These are some of the various forms of 'strawberry' terminal (Plates 13a, ii; 13b, i; 16b, i) made at Leeds before 1775, but other variations of it were made elsewhere.

Fig. 10: 4, 5, page 153. These terminals are indicative of Leeds manufacture of both the early and later periods, as they do not appear to have been used by any other factory.

Fig. 10: 6, page 153. This terminal occurs on some early Leeds creamware.

Fig. 10: 11, page 153. This is by far the most usual Leeds terminal used on

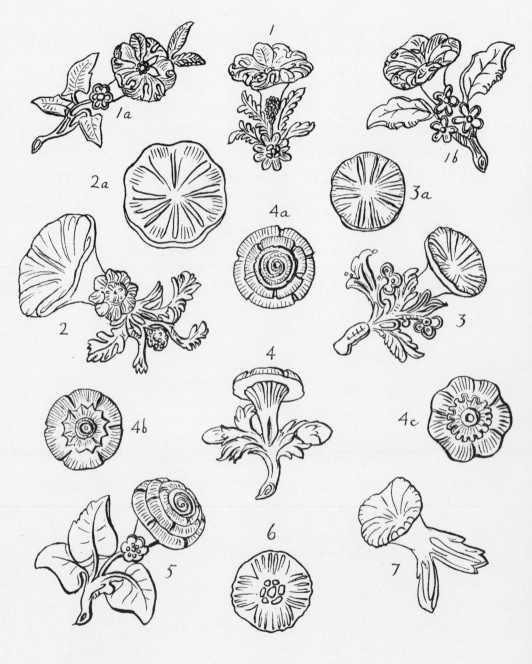

Fig. 9

Fig. 10

creamware after 1775 (Plate 27a and many others). It also occurs on the red stoneware punch-kettle (Plate 2) and does not appear to have been used by any other
factory.

Fig. 10: 12, page 153. This terminal often occurs on chestnut baskets and
tureens made by the Leeds Pottery and is illustrated in the Drawing Books of the
Pottery.

Fig. 10: 13, page 153. This terminal (Plates 15, 27b, ii; colour plate facing
page 38) was frequently used by the Leeds Pottery on creamware made both before
and after 1775. It also occurs on the Leeds red earthenware mug (Plate 1), and does
not appear to have been used by other factories.

Fig. 10: 17, page 153. This terminal occurs on both the Leeds creamware teapot (Plate 32a) and on the saltglaze sauce-boat (Plate 5a).

Fig. 10: 16, page 153. Though this terminal (Plate 26b, i, ii) occurs on Leeds
creamware, it is also to be found on teapots of the 'Prodigal Son' group engraved
by William Greatbatch, which are not all of Leeds manufacture (page 39).

Fig. 10: 9, 10, 14, 15, page 153. These terminals occur on small pieces of
Leeds creamware such as cups (Plate 13b, ii) and cream-jugs, and are illustrated
in the Leeds Drawing Books.

CHAPTER ELEVEN

Other Local Potteries

EARTHENWARE FACTORIES in England during the eighteenth century were for the most part situated in groups. There were the Liverpool potteries, the Tyne-side potteries, the potteries of the Wear, the Staffordshire potteries, the Bristol potteries and so on. The reason for the grouping was the presence in certain localities of natural resources of value to the manufacture of pottery, combined with the existence of good waterways to facilitate the transport of both the raw materials and manufactured products. Such conditions were to be found in South Yorkshire, where a considerable group of potteries established themselves along the River Humber and its tributaries the Rivers Aire, Calder, and Don. Of these the Leeds Pottery was not only the largest, but one of the oldest and was closely connected by family and business relationships with others in the area, some of which were formed by former apprentices to the Leeds Pottery. Some notes on these potteries are therefore essential in order to present a true picture of the Leeds Pottery itself.

POTTERIES OF THE DON

Swinton Pottery. This was first established in 1745 by Edward Butler whose chief product, according to Jewitt, was brown saltglazed stoneware similar to that made at Nottingham and elsewhere. Jewitt in his *Ceramic Art of Great Britain* illustrates a posset-pot of this ware authenticated as having been made at the Swinton Pottery and dated 1759. In 1765 the works passed into the hands of William Malpass, who held another small pot-works at Kilnhurst and continued the same production. In 1778 Thomas Bingley became a principal partner of the works with Malpass, and the firm was carried on under the name 'Thomas Bingley & Co.', when various types of ware were made.

In 1787 the Swinton Pottery virtually became a branch of the Leeds Pottery; John and Joshua Green and William Hartley being the principal partners of both. At this time the Swinton Pottery was styled 'Greens, Hartley & Co.', whereas the Leeds Pottery traded under the name 'Hartley, Greens & Co.' Pieces that can be attributed to the Swinton Pottery during its connexion with the Leeds Pottery are very few. Kidson says, 'for business reasons creamware was principally made at the Leeds Pottery; a more decorated class of goods being manufactured at the Swinton factory'. This seems to be most likely, especially in view of the fact that the Leeds Pottery must have sent large quantities of creamware to Swinton, since one finds repeated statements of 'ordered to Swinton' in the Leeds order books (page 55), and it is evident that the Swinton factory used a pattern book which contained many identical plates to the Leeds Pattern Book (page 56). This is corroborated by Jewitt, who had evidently seen one, as he says, 'the Leeds heading was cut off and "Greens, Bingley & Co. Swinton Pottery" substituted in ink'. After 1796 the Pottery issued a price list headed 'Greens, Bingley & Co. Swinton Pottery, make, sell and export wholesale, all sorts of Earthenware, viz: Cream-coloured or Queen's, Nankeen Blue, Tortoise Shell, Fine Egyptian Black, Brown China, etc. Also the above sorts enamelled, printed or ornamented with gold or silver.' This list further bears out Kidson's statement.

All connexions between the Leeds and Swinton Potteries ceased in 1806, probably consequent on the death of John Green the previous year. At the final meeting of partners at the Swinton Pottery there were present William Hartley, Ebenezer Green, and George Hanson for the Leeds Pottery; and Thomas Bingley, John Brameld, and William Brameld for the Swinton Pottery.

From 1806 John and William Brameld seem to have been sole proprietors, as the firm from that date traded under the name 'Brameld & Co. Swinton Pottery', during which time some fine green-glazed and other wares were made, the mark used being BRAMELD in capital letters followed by a cross and sometimes a number. After the death of William Brameld in 1813, Thomas, George, and John Brameld, sons of the previous partners, succeeded to the business which in 1826 became the Rockingham China Works.

The Don Pottery. Both Jewitt and Kidson state that this Pottery was founded in 1790 by a John Green who was related to John Green of the Leeds Pottery, and that he had previously been manager to both the Leeds and Swinton factories. It is quite clear however from Letter 3 (page 163) that the Don Pottery was in fact founded by John and William Green who were sons of John Green of the Leeds Pottery. Hurst in his *Catalogue of the Boynton Collection* states that the Directory of 1833 gives the date of the first establishment of this Pottery as 1801. On the 5th January 1805 the *Leeds Mercury* published the following notice: 'On Wednesday last died Mr John Green, one of the Proprietors of the Don Pottery near Doncaster and formerly a partner in the extensive pottery near this town' (page 167). This makes it clear that some time before 1805 John Green of the Leeds Pottery had resigned his connexions there and had become a proprietor of the Don Pottery with his two sons. In 1807 the Don Pottery first traded under the name 'Greens, Clark & Co.' Previous to this the name was 'Green, Don Pottery'. In 1822 the Pottery traded under the name 'John and William Green & Co.' It is therefore clear that the Leeds and Don Potteries were very closely connected by family ties. In 1838 the Don Pottery was sold to Samuel Barker and was not finally closed till 1893.

The marks were DON POTTERY, or GREEN DON POTTERY impressed, or DON POTTERY pencilled in red. The marks of Barker consisted of a lion supporting a standard with the word DON inscribed on it, the word POTTERY below, and in some cases the word BARKER above. Another mark was the word DON within a cartouche.

The Don Pottery issued a pattern book on the same lines as that of the Leeds Pottery and a list headed 'Greens, Clark & Co., Don Pottery, near Doncaster, Make, Sell and Export wholesale all the various kinds of Earthenware, viz: Cream-colour, Brown, Blue and Green, Shell, Nankeen Blue, Printed, Painted and Enamelled, Egyptian Black, Brown China, Etc., etc. Also Services executed in Borders, Landscapes, Coats of Arms, etc., and ornamented with Gold or Silver.'

The ware though often pleasing was considerably inferior to the Leeds productions. One of the most successful products of the Don Pottery was a whiteware enamelled with flowers copied from herbals with the name of the flower painted on the back and impressed DON POTTERY. This type of ware was of course produced by many factories including the Leeds Pottery.

In addition to the list of wares advertised in the pattern book Jewitt records that the Don Pottery made porcelain between 1810 and 1812.

Hurst recounts that when John Green first started the Don Pottery he took the models as prepared to a man named Newton, who had a small enamel kiln at the back of his house, to be fired. Newton would probably be a decorator.

Other potteries on the Don were:

Newhill Pottery founded in 1822 by Joseph Twigg, late manager of the Swinton Pottery. White and printed earthenware were produced. The mark was TWIGG NEWHILL impressed.

Mexborough. There were a number of potteries founded at Mexborough during the nineteenth century. The earliest of these was the Mexborough Old Pottery established in 1800 by Sowter & Bromley, who chiefly produced printed ware. The mark was SOWTER & CO. MEXBRO impressed.

Kilnhurst Old Pottery was established in 1746, probably by William Malpass, who was also at the Swinton factory in 1765; about 1800 it was worked by Hawley, who also had a pottery at Rawmarsh. In 1822 the firm was Turner & Hawley; in 1838 it was worked by George Green and in 1839 it passed into the hands of Joseph Twigg & Brothers, also of Newhill. They are said to have made 'White and Ivory earthenware, printed, painted, sponged, banded, mosaic, etc.'[1]

Templehurst. Traces of a creamware factory here have been recently reported.

POTTERIES OF THE AIRE

Large-scale nineteenth-century maps of the Leeds district show a great many potteries in this area. Like the Leeds Pottery itself, most of these were situated on the south side of the River Aire. Some only produced common or sanitary earthenware and do not now concern us, but there were others which made fine earthenware and were working in the eighteenth century, and although little is known of their productions the following notes may be of interest.

Rothwell Pottery. This pottery was situated three miles south-west of the Leeds Pottery. Judging by the advertisements for its sale it must have been an important factory, yet nothing is known of its products. It was worked by John Smith and some partners from some time before 1770 in which year it was put up for sale (page 168). Although at the sale there was much material for the manufacturing of creamware or saltglaze the emphasis of the pottery seems to have been on enamelling, as we see from the advertisement in the *Leeds Mercury* for April 13th, 1773, which states that three spacious rooms were fitted up for Enamel work and a small pan for grinding enamel colours. John Platt writing in 1772 says: 'At Rothwell valuing Building & Stock of J. Smith ye Painter and three more partners of a Pottery at Rothwell near Leeds which they gave up the works not answering. . . .'

It is more than likely that some of the Leeds creamware was sent to Rothwell to be enamelled, and it may be that after David Rhodes went to London in 1768 the Leeds Pottery commenced its own enamelling and John Smith may have suffered in consequence. One cannot help speculating as to whether, after the sale of the Rothwell Pottery in 1774, John Smith went to the Leeds Pottery as a principal enameller and modeller, since a Leeds figure of a flute-player (Plate 38) is inscribed 'John Smith 1797' (Fig. 6: 31, page 35).

The Pottery was acquired in 1774 by Samuel Shaw from Staffordshire, who made and sold 'all sorts of cream colour, red, yellow[2] and painted wares at his new

---

[1] Arthur Hurst, *Catalogue of the Boynton Collection*.
[2] The 'red' and 'yellow' probably refers to earthenware of the so-called Astbury type.

pottery at Rothwell' (page 169). Samuel Shaw died in 1776 and the Pottery was again put up for sale.

Hunslet Hall or Petty's Pottery. This pottery was between five and six hundred yards south-west of the Leeds Pottery (map, Fig. 1, page 6). Kidson, writing of this pottery in 1892 states, 'The premises still stand in as ruinous a condition as the Old Leeds Pottery. It is situated at the corner of Beeston Road and Holbeck Moor, but just within the township of Hunslet.[1] After the Leeds Old Pottery, it was in its day the most important of the local potteries.' It was founded by Petty and Rainforth in 1757, according to the testimony of Petty's son (page 163), who also tells us that Rainforth had previously served his apprenticeship with the Greens at the Leeds Pottery. About 1792 it became Rainforth & Co. In 1818 Pettys & Co.; in 1822 Petty & Hewitt; in 1825 Samuel Petty & Son; in 1847 John Mills; in 1867 Mills Brothers, and was finally closed in 1880. Creamware was the principal product. In view of the fact that Rainforth was apprenticed to the Greens it is probable that the ware was very like that produced by the Leeds Pottery. None of the early pieces made by this pottery has yet been identified, but several pieces with the impressed marked 'Rainforth & Co.' are known,[2] but if these can be taken as typical examples of the Pottery, the ware was decidedly inferior to that produced by the Leeds Pottery.

Taylor's Pottery or New Pottery was in Jack Lane, Hunslet (map, Fig. 1, page 6), less than half a mile south-east of the Leeds Pottery, and was established during the eighteenth century, but the first information we have of it is in 1847, when it was being worked by William Taylor. Painted and blue-printed wares were produced.

Allison's Pottery was in the same yard as the New Pottery in Jack Lane. In 1809 it was being worked by Joseph Allison and in 1828 by John Allison. It is thought that coarse earthenwares were its only production.

Meadow Lane Pottery or *Russell's Pottery* on the corner of Jack Lane and Meadow Lane a few hundred yards west of the Leeds Pottery was being worked in 1809 by William Russell for the production of blackware (map, Fig. 1, page 6).

Marsden's Pottery was in Bedford Row, Hunslet. Kidson states that John Marsden in about 1835 made figures and mantelpiece ornaments as well as, so he believed, figures of horses similar to those made by the Leeds Pottery.

---

[1] This position is in accord with a map of 1832 and is where it is shown on Fig. 1, page 6 of this book. A map surveyed in 1846–7 and engraved in 1852, however, names this pottery 'Victoria Pottery' and names the pottery immediately south of Hunslet Hall (Fig. 1, page 6) 'Hunslet Hall Pottery'. It would seem that the names of these two potteries became interchanged on the later map.

[2] Fitzwilliam Museum, Victoria and Albert Museum, Yorkshire Museum.

Leathley Lane Pottery was situated east of the Leeds Pottery, which it practically adjoined. In 1828 it was worked by Reuben John and John North. In 1830 it was named the Leeds Union Pottery. The early wares of this pottery are not known, but according to Kidson they were probably on the lines of those produced by Samuel Wainwright at the Leeds Pottery. From 1893 the pottery was known as the Leeds Art Pottery Company and produced ornamental wares, (map, Fig. 1, page 6).

Swillington Bridge Pottery about five miles south-east of Leeds on the River Aire at Woodlesford was being worked in 1797 by William Taylor and in 1805 by William and Thomas Wildblood. A good-quality creamware plaque with figures moulded in relief and marked 'John Wildblood, Swillington Bridge Pottery July 12, 1831' was presented by J. R. Kidson to Oxley Grabham, who illustrates it in his book *Yorkshire Potteries*, Fig. 100. This pottery is also known to have made blackware. A stamp for marking ware having on it a crown in relief was discovered a few years ago amongst some of the masonry during repairs to Swillington Bridge.

The wares made by the *Holbeck Moor Pottery* worked by Joseph Dennison (page 165) in Elland Road, about half a mile south-west of the Leeds Pottery, and a pottery at *Hunslet Moor* worked by Thomas Cartledge in 1818 are not known. It may be that pieces of creamware bearing the impressed mark HM (Fig. 6: 39, page 145) were made at one or other of these potteries (map, Fig. 1, page 6).

It is interesting to note that Hurst in his catalogue to the Boynton Collection states that in 1828 Joseph Warburton was a china and glass enameller and gilder at 47 Meadow Lane, which was close to the Leeds Pottery.

The Castleford Pottery was an important creamware factory about eight miles south-east of Leeds and was founded about 1790 by David Dunderdale who served his apprenticeship at the Leeds Pottery. It produced its own Pattern Book and became noted for white felspathic stoneware. The wares were sometimes marked CASTLEFORD POTTERY or D.D. & Co. but were inferior to those of the Leeds Pottery.

Ferrybridge Pottery near the Castleford Pottery was founded in 1792 by Wm. Tomlinson & Co. Before 1804 it was known as the Knottingly Pottery. The wares made include creamware, green-glazed, white saltglaze and jasper ware. The marks were WEDGWOOD & CO. or FERRYBRIDGE.

Belle Vue Pottery, at Hull on the River Humber was established in 1802 by James and Jeremiah Smith. The creamware produced was often transfer-printed but was inferior to that of the Leeds Pottery.

Letters, Extracts and Indentures

A. LETTERS

Pasted into a copy of the first edition (1783) of the Pattern Book which formerly belonged to Sir Henry de la Bèche, Director of the Museum of Practical Geology, Jermyn Street, London, and now in the Victoria and Albert Museum Library, are the following letters written by Thomas Wilson of Leeds and sent to Sir Henry de la Bèche in 1854. These letters were the source of information for the first histories of the Leeds Pottery and their significance is discussed in the first chapter of the present book.

(*Letter 1*)
Crimbles House, Leeds.
20 March 1854.

Sir,

I fear there will be more difficulty than I at first anticipated in getting information about the Leeds Pottery—and certainly more delay than I hoped—in consequence of the great distance of time since its first establishment and of its having passed by the misfortunes of the proprietors into new hands—All the original specimens of the ware, and most of any antiquity have been dispersed and all the books and papers that remain are in the hands of the official Assignee. The present proprietor to whom I have obtained an introduction professes to be disposed to give you every assistance in his power—but is at present very much engaged. He has promised however to get the old papers, and to collect all the information he can from old workmen as well as to try and get some specimens of the original ware.

Under these circumstances I think the best course would be, if you would have the kindness to state specifically what kind of information you more particularly and immediately want and what other particulars you would wish to ascertain—and I will direct the party's attention to the more important points first and then endeavour afterwards to procure the remainder. Without this knowledge of your wants we may probably waste a good deal of time in looking after curious matter that you care nothing about, and omit what is essentially useful to you.

I understand the Pottery was first established in 1760 by two brothers of the name of Green—that they first made a black ware and subsequently a cream coloured ware—that about 1790 they carried on a large trade with Russia, having almost a monopoly of that market—on account of their goods standing the climate remarkably well—that they were subsequently driven out by the lighter manufacture of Wedgwood—I have also seen a copy of an Agreement in 1775 between the Greens and a Miller in the neighbourhood by which Greens were to be permitted to put up a wheel in his mill for grinding their flints—which also states the price they were to pay.

I am told also the Potteries at Castleford & Knottingly—the former still in work—were established about the same time as those at Leeds.

The present proprietor has a few old cups and plates—the ground of a bluish white colour—the pattern a dullish blue or green—the weight of the piece, is very great and the glaze not very good—but the owner has no clue to the date—they have also Books of Patterns without date—but on looking at the paper I found it had the watermark of 1814.

This is all I have been able to collect—but what I should wish to know is whether these specimens or books—if they can be obtained—would be of any value—also whether you wish for a list of the several owners of the Pottery—and of the kinds of ware made—and also the quantity manufactured in a year—and whether you wish enquiry to be made respecting Castleford and Knottingly Potteries—and to what extent—

I am, Sir,
Yours faithfully
Thomas Wilson

Sir H. J. De La Bèche.

(*Letter 2*)

Crimbles House, Leeds.
26 May 1854.

My dear Sir,

I am sorry that I have not been able to send you answer to your inquiries about the Leeds Potteries earlier and that even now they are so meagre. I will however persue the inquiry this autumn, when I hope to be more at leisure, and if I meet with anything worth recording, I will not fail to let you know. The fact is the history of the Leeds Pottery is like that of many of our earlier Manufacturing establishments, it attained a certain degree of reputation and extent of trade at one period, which was not maintained at a later period and by the subsequent proprietors. In 1815 the estate passed into the hands of Assignees,[1] and all papers and books connected with its early career seem then to have been dispersed. This has been the cause of the great difficulty I have found in getting any accurate information. I am indebted for the principal part of what I now send you to Mr. William Warburton, son of one of the present proprietors and if you name your authorities he is the party who should be mentioned.

Have you any account of the Wortley Fire Brick Manufacture? These bricks though inferior to Stourbridge are extensively used in Iron Furnaces and in setting Engine Boilers —there is also at Farnley a manufacture of Terra Cotta in Vases, Chimney Pots etc. etc.

I am Dear Sir
Yours truly
Thomas Wilson

Sir H. T. De la Bèche.

[1] This took place in 1820, not 1815.

Enclosed with this letter was the following questionnaire with answers supplied by William Warburton.

1 Date of first establishment	1 1760
2 Clays first employed whether from the vicinity or otherwise	2 Cornwall & Dorsetshire
3 Character of first manufactured ware	3 Fancy & Cream coloured
4 Names of those who founded or were early engaged in the manufacture	4 & 5
5 An account of the different changes in proprietors afterwards	Humble, Green & Co. Hartley Greens & Co. Sam.' Wainwright S & S Chappell Warburton & Britton
6 When Poole Clays first introduced	6 1760
7 When Flints first employed	7
8 Any information connected with the supply or use of Poole clay or Flints	8 Ever since the pottery was established Poole clay must have been used.
9 Information connected with changes in the manufacture & character of the ware	9 The ware was very inferior to that of the present time.
10 Situation of the first Works also situation of other than the first Works	10 On the present site. Others in the immediate neighbourhood.
11 Dates when any may have been discontinued	11 All are still working.
12 If any present Works	12 Yes
13 Materials which may now be employed	13 Too numerous to mention
14 Any general information which may be thought calculated to contribute to the History of the Leeds Potteries	14
15 Marks for the Ware	15 Various at the present time.

WILLIAM WARBURTON

(*Letter 3*)

Crimbles House, Leeds.
27 May 1854.

My dear Sir,

In addition to Mr Warburton's answer to your enquiries I have gleaned the following particulars.

From Mr Petty, son of a Mr Petty, who in conjunction with one Rainforth, an apprentice of the Greens established an adjoining Pottery in 1757.

Green's first ware was black—afterwards Cream coloured—John Green was father of John and William Green who founded the Don Pottery at Swinton. The Leeds Pottery had at one time all the trade to Russia—say 3,000 or 4,000 pieces a year.

A Mr Barwick was their Agent in Russia and then his nephew—Jubb.

Ruperti was their first foreign handler—afterwards a partner. I give you these names because you may meet with them elsewhere.

The Potteries at Castleford and Knottingly were established a few years later than the Leeds Pottery in consequence of its success.

From Mr W. M. Maude.

It was Hartley, Greens & Co. who carried on the large business in Russia and had the Command of the market till Wedgwood superseded them.

Their Ware stood the climate particularly well.

About 1790 John Green had a quarrel with the Navigation about the Dues on Flints—and in consequence had them carried up the Wharfe to Tadcaster—there by Land to Thorpe Arch where they were ground—and then carted 14 miles to Leeds!

I have met amongst the Title Deeds of Flint Mills with a draft of the following agreement—which I have no doubt was executed as the Flint grinding is carried on there to this day—

1775 November 11th, 'Joshua Green of Middleton Gent & John Green of Hunslet, Potter, with divers others under the firm of Humble Green & Co.' agree with Hutchinson & Evers of Flint Mills as follows—Greens were to put up at Flint Mills and Keep in repair a Water Wheel with all necessary machinery for grinding Flints—the wheel only to be used by Greens for 13 years. Greens were also to find a man to manage the business, and as much *whole* burnt Flint as could be ground—and to pay 10s. for every 100 Pecks of well ground and levigated flints, the Workmen's wages not exceeding 3s. being finally deducted. At the end of 13 years Greens were to be at liberty to take away the Flint pan and everything except the Water Wheel and Cog Wheel.

Of course you are aware of what is said by Marryatt on the subject at p. 65 of his work.

I am dear Sir,
Yours sincerely
Thomas Wilson.

Sir H. T. De la Bèche.

B. EXTRACTS

(1) *Leeds Intelligencer*, 12 May 1761

'Robinson and Rhodes, opposite the George in Briggate, Leedes. Enamel and Burn in Colours and Gold, Foreign and English China; and match broken Sets of enamell'd China Tea Ware, with Foreign or English and make them compleat to any Pattern requir'd, either *India* or *Dresden*. They also enamell Coats of Arms &c. and sell a good Assortment of Foreign China, and great Variety of useful English China, of the newest Improvement, which they engage to wear as well as Foreign, and will change gratis, if broke with hot Water. They also enamell Stoneware, as cheap as in Staffordshire, and sell all Sorts of fine Earthenware, likewise piece all sorts of *India* Tea Ware, by melting it together in the Fire, so as to render it as useful, without rivetting, and to ring as well as before it was broken. Ready Money or Goods for broken Flint Glass.'

Note. A slightly shorter advertisement to the same effect was printed in the *Leeds Intelligencer* of 28 October 1760 (*English Cream-coloured Earthenware*, p. 18).

(2) *Leeds Intelligencer*, 26 May 1761

'To be sold

'A Close of Land in Hunslet in the Parish of Leedes situate on the West Side of the Lane leading from Leedes to Holbeck and divided from the South side of Major Judson's Garden by Gain Lane, the said Close is Freehold, contains near four Acres and is now in the Occupation of Mr. Joshua Green; For further Particulars enquire of Messrs Thomas and Edward Prince, in Meadow Lane, Leedes.'

(3) *Leeds Mercury*, 7 March 1769

'To be Lett to enter to immediately situate at Holbeck near Leeds. The Pot-Works Warehouses and a good House adjoining in the occupation of Mr. Joseph Dennison the Owner, of whom further particulars may be had.'

Note. This presumably refers to the Holbeck Moor Pottery (map, Fig. 1, page 6).

(4) *Leeds Mercury*, 28 August 1770

'Last Tuesday a misfortune happened at the large Earthenware manufactory now erecting near this town, owing, as we are informed, to one of the master bricklayers hurrying up one of the tall hovels (as they are called) too expeditiously, by which the top fell in just when finished, and drove two men and two boys before it.

'The boys were immediately carried to our Infirmary and one of them called Moses Hawkhead soon expired; the other we hear is likely to do well. Richard Holmby, one of the men, it is thought cannot recover.'

Note. A somewhat similar notice was published in the *Leeds Intelligencer* of the same date.

(5) *Leeds Mercury*, 4 October 1774

'On Wednesday died in childbed Mrs Green wife of Saville Green of the Pottery near this town.'

Note. Saville Green was first cousin to John Green.

(6) *Leeds Mercury*, 30 July 1776

'Run away. Thomas Sykes apprentice to Humble, Hartley, Greens and Co. of the Leeds Pottery . . .'

Note. On 11 November 1775 the firm traded under Humble, Green & Co.

(7) *Leeds Mercury*, 20 May 1777

'A few days ago was married Mr Hartley of the Pottery in this town to Miss Booth of Park Hill near Bradford.'

(8) *Leeds Intelligencer*, 20 February 1781

'Notice is hereby given that the Partnership in the Leeds Pottery between Richard Humble, William Hartley, Joshua Green, John Green, Henry Ackroyd, John Barwick, Saville Green and Samuel Wainwright under the firm *Humble, Hartley, Greens & Company* is amicably dissolved and that the said William Hartley, Joshua Green, John Green, Henry Ackroyd,

John Barwick, Saville Green and Samuel Wainwright, will hereafter trade under the firm of *Hartley, Greens & Company*.

Richard Humble	Henry Ackroyd
William Hartley	John Barwick
Joshua Green	Saville Green
John Green	Samuel Wainwright'

(9) *Leeds Intelligencer*, 12 February 1788

'Last Tuesday morning the Leeds Pottery belonging to Messrs. Hartley, Greens & Co. accidentally took fire, and before it was got under several warehouses full of earthenware, and the workshops, utensils and sundry articles were destroyed, the loss in property is supposed to be above £2000.'

(10) *Leeds Intelligencer*, 15 April 1788

'Tuesday last died, Mr Henry Ackroyd, one of the proprietors of the Pottery in this town.'

(11) *Leeds Intelligencer*, 13 January 1789

'On Monday last was married the Rev. Mr Parsons, Minister of the White Chapel, to Miss Akeroyd, daughter of the late Mr Akeroyd, one of the proprietors of the pottery, both of this town.'

(12) *Diary of John Platt of Rotherham* (*E.C.C. Transactions*, vol. 5, part 3, page 172. A. J. B. Kiddell)

'19th of January 1791—At Leeds Pottery Measuring and Valuing Buildings etc. for Messrs. Hartley & Green, to February 27th at ye Pottery, flint mills, and other works there valuing 34 days.

'10th October 1791—Finished ye Valuation of the Leeds Pottery to Mr. Calvert amounts to £53,860. 14s. 8¾d.'

(13) *Leeds Intelligencer*, 27 August 1792

'On Tuesday died at an advanced age Mrs Green, Mother of Mr John Green of the Pottery in this town.'

Note. Presumably Joshua the elder brother had already died, as he is not mentioned here.

(14) *Leeds Intelligencer*, 14 March 1796

'On Friday se'nnight died aged 88, Mrs Green, mother of Mr Saville Green of the Pottery near this town.'

(15) *Leeds Intelligencer*, 10 April 1797

'On Wednesday morning died Mrs Hartley the wife of Mr Hartley of the Pottery in this town.'

(16) *Leeds Intelligencer*, 30 April 1798

'On Saturday died Mr Wainwright of Ferrybridge, the postmaster of that place and one of the partners in the Leeds Pottery.'

Note. This was Thomas Wainwright.

(17) *Leeds Intelligencer*, 24 February 1800

'On Thursday last was married at Preston in Lancashire, William Hartley Esquire of the Pottery near this town to Mrs Hayes of the former place.'

(18) *Leeds Mercury*, 5 May 1804

'On Sunday died Mr Matthew Wright thirty four years one of the principal workmen at Messrs. Hartley, Greens & Co's Pottery.'

Note. Matthew Wright would have been first employed in 1770, the year when the new extension was built.

(19) *Leeds Mercury*, 6 October 1804

'Advertisement of Sale by Auction of two Twentieth shares in the Leeds Pottery the Property of a Gentleman residing abroad.'

Note. This was probably Saville Green (see extract number 25).

(20) *Leeds Mercury*, 5 January 1805

'On Wednesday last died Mr John Green—one of the Proprietors of the Don Pottery near Doncaster and formerly a partner in the extensive pottery near this town.'

(21) *Leeds Mercury*, 16 August 1817

'On Tuesday last at Rothwell Church Mr Thomas Craven a painter at the Leeds Pottery to Miss Coultate both of this town, after a tedious courtship of 28 years 6 months and 6 days.'

(22) *Leeds Intelligencer*, 20 September 1819

'On Tuesday last aged 29, Mr James Scott of the Leeds Pottery, a Wesleyan local Preacher.'

(23) *London Gazette*, 6 June 1820

'Mary Ackroyd of Leeds in the County of York, Earthenware Manufacturer, Dealer and Chapwoman, and she being declared a Bankrupt is hereby required to surrender herself to the Commissioners in the said Commission named on the 26th day of June instant.'

Note. A similar notice appeared in the *London Gazette* of the same day commencing 'Ebenezer Green of Leeds . . .' Both Mary Ackroyd and Ebenezer Green were partners in the Leeds Pottery at that time.

(24) *Leeds Intelligencer*, 10 July 1820

'In Ebenezer Green's Bankruptcy

'The Creditors who have proved their Debts under a Commission of Bankrupt awarded and issued forth against Ebenezer Green of Leeds in the County of York, Earthenware Manufacturer, Dealer and Chapman, are desired to meet the Assignees of the said Bankrupt's Estate and Effects, at the Office of Messrs. Smith and Moore, Solicitors, Leeds, on Saturday, the Fifteenth Day of July Instant at Eleven o'Clock in the Forenoon, to assent to or dissent from the said Assignees commencing prosecuting or defending any Suit or Suits at Law, or in Equity, for the Recovery of any Part of the said Bankrupt's Estate or Effects, or to the compounding, submitting to Arbitration, giving Time to Debtors, and taking Security or otherwise agreeing any Matter or Thing relating thereto; and also to agree to, or dissent from, the said Assignees employing an Accountant to arrange the said Bankrupt's Accounts, and collect and get in the Debts due to his Estate; and to their making such Accountant such Compensation for the same as to them shall seem proper; and to assent to or dissent from, the said Assignees selling by Private Contract by a Valuation, or otherwise, the Shares and Interest which the said Bankrupt had, at the time he became a Bankrupt, in an Earthenware Manufactory at Hunslet, in the County of York, which the said Bankrupt, was then carrying on in Copartnership with several other Persons, under the Firm of Messrs. Hartley, Greens, and Co. And also to assent to or dissent from the said Assignees selling the Household Furniture, Implements of Household and other personal Estate and Effects of the said Bankrupt, for ready money, or upon Credit or otherwise, as the said Assignees may deem expedient and proper; and also to assent to, or dissent from, the said Assignees making an Allowance to the said Bankrupt for his Maintenance, and for any Services he may be employed in by the said Assignees, and on other special Business—By Order, Smith and Moore, Solicitors for the Assignees, Leeds, 5th July, 1820.'

Note. A similar notice appeared in the *Leeds Intelligencer* under the same date commencing 'Mary Ackroyd . . .' Other notices of the bankruptcy appeared in the *Leeds Mercury* of 3 June, 10 June, 3 July and 18 July. Also in the *London Gazette* of 11 July. There are further references to it at the Public Record Office in Index 22669, Docket Book 1819, vol. 36, Court of Bankruptcy. These give the date of the Docket as 27 May 1820, and the date of the Commission 30 May 1820.

(25) *Leeds Intelligencer*, 2 October 1820

'On the 14th of July at Rio de Janeiro, Saville Green Esquire, one of the proprietors of the Leeds Pottery.'

(26) *Leeds Intelligencer*, 31 August 1826

'On Saturday last at Bramham, Mr Robert Atkinson, surgeon of Thorpe Arch to Miss Green of the same place, daughter of the late Saville Green Esquire of the Leeds Pottery.'

(27) *Leeds Intelligencer*, 12 July 1827

'On Saturday at an advanced age Mr Ebenezer Green of this town formerly in the firm of Hartley, Greens & Co. of the Leeds Potteries.'

Notices Concerning the Rothwell Pottery

(28) *Leeds Mercury*, 29 May 1770

'Rothwell Potworks

'One third share of Rothwell Potworks to be disposed of. Any person intending to purchase, may apply to Mr Smith at Rothwell, one of the proprietors.'

(29) *Leeds Mercury*, 13 April 1773

'Rothwell Potworks, in the county of York, situated within 4 miles from Leeds and 5 from Wakefield, 1 mile from the turnpike road leading to Wakefield and within a small distance of the navigable rivers, Aire and Calder, the neighbourhood of which pottery abounds with a great variety of clay and coal. The buildings consist of a large hovel containing 3 kilns, with all proper conveniences; two large warehouses, and other convenient houses, for carrying on the pottery business in the most commodious and extensive manner, wherein are a large quantity of Devonshire clays, and all tools and utensils necessary for workmen, with a great variety of working moulds in the newest taste.

'All the buildings open into a spacious yard, also several dwelling houses for workmen contiguous, together with a new erected flint mill, which works one pan of 15 feet, one of 5, and another of 3 feet diameter. Also a small pan for grinding of Enamel colours, and a pair of stones for grinding of plaister, clays etc. with conveniences for erecting a machine for slip and beating of clay. A dwelling house for the flint grinder, and 3 spacious rooms, well lighted and fitted up, for the Enamel work, and 2 reservoirs wherein are 2500 pecks of ground flint, and about 9 acres of very good meadow ground adjoining the flint mill.

'The whole of the said buildings and grounds are held by lease for the term of 21 years. Which lease with the clays, utensils, moulds, and materials and a stock of ware on the premises are intended to be sold to the best bidders on Tuesday, the 22nd day of June next between the hours of 3 and 6 in the afternoon, at the house of Mrs Cooke, the Old King's Arms, in Leeds, according to conditions then and there to be produced unless before sold by private contract, of which timely notice will be given. For further particulars enquire of Thomas Fenton Esq., of Rothwell Haigh, and Mr Thomas Walker of the Glass House, both in the parish of Rothwell, and Mr Samuel Keeling of Rothwell, aforesaid, to whom John Smith & Company, the late proprietors of the said Pottery have assigned the same, together with the rest of their copartnership effects, in trust for the benefit of their partnership creditors, and all such persons as do now stand indebted to the same copartnership are desired forthwith to pay the same to the said trustees, or they will be sued forthwith without further notice.

'And for a view of the premises to be sold enquire at the Pottery.

'The works are carried on, and the warehouse open for sale, as usual.'

Note. The pottery was not sold on this occasion, but at a sale held on the 7 May 1774.

(30) *Leeds Mercury,* 21 June 1774
'A New Pottery
'This is to inform the public that Samuel Shaw of Rothwell, potter (late from Staffordshire), makes and sells all sorts of cream colour, red, yellow, and painted wares at his new pottery in Rothwell, where tradesmen and others may depend on being served at the very lowest prices, wholesale and retail.'

(31) *Diary of John Platt of Rotherham*
   (from a paper read by A. J. B. Kiddell, *E.C.C. Transactions,* vol. 5, part 3, page 172)
'8th Dec. to 15, 1772. At Rothwell valuing Building & Stock of J. Smith ye Painter and three more partners of a Pottery at Rothwell near Leeds, which they gave up, the works not answering nor could they carry on without more capital spent—'
'9th March 1789—Jno Smith painter here from Duke of Portland's.'

Notice on the Rotherham Pottery

(32) *A Six Months Tour Through the North of England*
    Arthur Young, 1769, vol. I, page 124
'Rotherham—Besides the iron manufactory they have a pottery in which is made the white, cream-coloured (Staffordshire) and tortoiseshell earthenware. It employs about two or three and twenty men and forty boys.'
Note. The 'white' refers to saltglaze.

C. INDENTURES

(1) Extract from Indenture, 29 June 1758, registered at West Riding Registry of Deeds Wakefield, Book B.3
'This Indenture made the Twenty ninth day of June . . . in the year of our Lord One thousand Seven hundred and fifty eight Between James Armitage of Hunslet in the County of York Merchant, Benjamin Stirk of Addle in the said County Yeoman, Bartle Waugh of Leeds in the said County Carpenter, Thomas Abbott of the same place Cordwainer, Henry Ackroyd of the same place Yeoman, William Green of Hunslet aforesaid Yeoman, William Sedgfield of Chappell Allerton in the said County Clothier, John Ingle of the same place Mason, and George Watkinson of Knowstrop in the Parish of Leeds in the said county Gardiner, of the one part and Charles Brandling of Middleton in the Parish of Rothwell in the same County Esquire and Lord of the Manor of the same Middleton of the other part . . . hath contracted with divers persons proprietors of lands and grounds for the liberty of laying down a waggon way through the said lands and grounds and also with the said James Armitage, Benjamin Stirk, Bartle Waugh, Thomas Abbott, Henry Ackroyd, William Green, William Sedgfield, John Ingle, and George Watkinson for. . . . All that piece or parcel of ground lying at the east end of the White Cloth Hall in Leeds aforesaid abutting south upon a garden belonging to Mr William Chipping and North upon the said Casson Close and containing in length sixteen yards and in breadth about six yards. . . .'
Footnote. The White Cloth Hall which was rebuilt a number of times on different sites must at this time have stood near the position the North Midland Railway Station was to occupy at a later date (map, Fig. 1, page 6).

(2) Extract from Indenture of June 1758. West Riding Registry of Deeds, Wakefield, Book B.3
'Jeremiah Dixon Esquire doth Demise Lease sel and to farm lett unto the said Charles Brandling all that close of meadows or pasture ground with the appurtenances called Rushey Pasture containing 5 acres, 1 rood, and 20 perches with the stable or holm standing and also full liberty for the said Charles Brandling to make lay and place a waggon way. . . .'

(3) Indenture between Jeremiah Dixon and Richard Humble, 30 November 1770. West Riding Registry of Deeds, Wakefield, Book BM. 229/290
'Indenture of lease and release bearing date 11th and 12th November 1770 the lease being made between Jeremiah Dixon of Allerton Gledhow in the parish of Leeds in the County

of York Esquire of the one part and Richard Humble in the said County Gentleman of the other part and the release being made between the said Jeremiah Dixon and Mary his wife of the one part and the said Richard Humble of the other part and are of and concerning all that close of Meadow or pasture ground commonly called or known by the name of Rushey Pasture containing by estimation 5 acres 1 rood and 20 perches with the stable or holm standing in the said close which said premises are situate in the township of Hunslet in the said parish of Leeds and now in the possession Tenure or Occupation of Charles Brandling Esquire his under tenants or Assigns together with the Appurtenances which said indentures are witnessed by Thomas Barston the younger in the county of York, gent, and Philip Coultman his clerk.'

(4) A memorial of an indenture of 1799 written by Edmund Dawson in 1837

'A memorial of indenture of lease and release bearing dates 1799 between William Wrigglesworth of Middleton on the one part and Alexander Turner of Leeds of the other and the release made between William Wrigglesworth of the one part and William Hartley of Hunslet in the Parish of Leeds, gentleman, John Green of Hunslet, gentleman, Ebenezer Green, Liquor merchant, Devisee under the will and Testament of Joshua Green deceased, Sarah Ackroyd of Leeds widow, Mary Ackroyd which said Sarah and Mary Ackroyd with Ebenezer Green (in the right of his wife) are the surviving personal representatives of Henry Ackroyd late of Hunslet, gent deceased. John Barwick of Leeds surgeon, Savile Green of Hunslet, gent, Samuel Wainwright of Boston in Kerseymere printer and Jane his wife, George Hanson of Manchester merchant, Nathaniel Clayton of Newcastle upon Tyne, esquire, Joseph Humble of Middleton, John Humble of Newcastle upon Tyne, and Thomas Humble of Newcastle upon Tyne joint executors and residuary legatees of Richard Humble of the fourth part. Alexander Turner of the fifth part and both of and concerning all that close of meadow and pasture ground commonly called Rushey Pasture containing five acres and a half with the messuages, cottages, warehouses, shops and other buildings standing and being thereon.

'This memorial is required to be registered by me Edmund Dawson of Rothwell Haigh, coal agent, who am now one of the persons seized of the Hereditaments and premises comprized in the within written memorial.

'Edmund Dawson
'7 Aug. 1837.'

(5) A memorial of indenture between Richard Britton and William Warburton (son of Samuel Warburton), dated 1863, and presumably written after the death of Samuel Warburton when Britton became sole proprietor of the Pottery.

'A Memorial to be Registered pursuant to Act of Parliament of a certain Indenture bearing date the Eighteenth day of November one thousand eight hundred and sixty-three and made between Richard Britton of Hunslet in the parish of Leeds in the county of York Earthenware Manufacturer of the one part and William Henry Warburton of Hunslet in Leeds aforesaid Manufacturing Chemist of the other part Of and concerning All that close or parcel of Land situate in the Township of Hunslet in Leeds aforesaid called by the

name of Rushey Pasture containing by estimation five acres one rood and twenty perches
And also all that plot piece or parcel of ground being part or parcel of a close of land situate
in Hunslet aforesaid called the Windmill Close bounded on the East side thereof by a close
of Land formerly belonging to Matthew Russell Esquire on the West side thereof by a close
of Land now or lately belonging to William Waite on the North end thereof by the residue
of the same close and on the Southend thereof by the said close called Rushey Pasture and
containing by admeasurement and survey one acre two roods and four perches (be the
same more or less) which same close of Land was formerly known by the name of one of the
Dowbrigg or otherwise Dowbridge closes save and except a certain piece of Land containing
two thousand seven hundred and thirty nine square yards being the North East End of the
said close of Land called the Windmill Close and which was some time since sold to the
North Midland Railway Company And also all and every the Buildings and Erections now
standing and being upon the said closes or parcels of Land consisting of four Biscuit Ware
Kilns, seven Glazing Kilns, hardening and enamelling Kilns, Brick Kilns and Sheds,
Counting houses, Warehouses, Workshops, Steam Mills, Flint Mill, Grinding Mill, Dwel-
linghouses, Cottages, Stabling and Land adjoining And also three Cottages situate near
Hunslet Moor All which same premises were lately in the occupation of the said Samuel
Warburton and Richard Britton their undertenants or assigns but are now in the occupa-
tion of the said Richard Britton his undertenants or assigns and have been and are commonly
called or known by the name of the Leeds Old Pottery Together with the Steam Engines,
Machinery, and Fixtures belonging to the freehold of the said hereditaments and premises
And all other the hereditaments and premises granted and conveyed unto the said Richard
Britton and his heirs by an Indenture of the fifth day of June one thousand eight hundred
and fifty one Together with all additions thereto and all Sheds, Steam Engines, Boilers,
Grinding Machines, and all fixed working plant fixtures, and other things now in the said
hereditaments and premises and which are comprized and set forth in the Schedule there-
under written And all other additions Sheds, Steam Engines, Boilers fixtures, and Machinery
and all other articles and things in the nature of fixtures or trade appliances erected upon or
placed within or to be found attached or annexed to and forming part of the freehold of the
said hereditaments and premises And the appurtenances And which said Indenture as to the
due execution thereof by the said Richard Britton and William Henry Warburton is
witnessed by Arthur W. Blackburn Clerk to Mr. Blackburn Solicitor Leeds and Wm. B.
Craven Clerk to Mess. Upton and Goodall Solicitors Leeds.

Signed and Sealed in the presence of Arthur W. Blackburn

Richard Britton.

Bibliography

Sir Henry de la Bèche, *Catalogue of the Museum of Practical Geology, Jermyn Street, London*, 1st edition 1855, 2nd edition 1871.

Llewellyn Jewitt, *Ceramic Art of Great Britain*, London, 1st edition 1878, 2nd edition 1884.

Joseph and Frank Kidson, *Historical Notices of the Leeds Old Pottery*, Leeds 1892.

Maud Sellers, *Pottery, A History of the County of York* (Victoria County Histories, Vol. II, 1912).

Oxley Grabham, *Yorkshire Potteries, Pots and Potters*, York 1916.

Arthur Hurst, *Catalogue of the Boynton Collection of Yorkshire Pottery*, York 1922.

Donald Towner, *Handbook of Leeds Pottery*, Leeds, 1951.

Donald Towner, 'The Leeds Pottery, Jack Lane Hunslet', in *Transactions of the English Ceramic Circle*, Vol. III, Part IV, 1955.

Donald Towner, 'Some Creamware Comparisons' in *Transactions of the English Ceramic Circle*, Vol. IV, Part 3, 1957.

Donald Towner, 'The Leeds Pottery and its Wares', Parts I to IV, *Apollo*, London, December 1956, February, March, and May 1957.

Donald Towner, *English Cream-coloured Earthenware*, London, 1957.

Index

ABBOTT, Thomas, 170
Ackroyd, Henry, 9, 10, 14, 16, 17, 165–6, 168, 170–1
Ackroyd, Mary, 11, 17, 20, 166–7, 171
Ackroyd, Sarah, 11, 17, 171
acorn knobs, 24
agate ware, 47, 147
Aire, River, 5, 12, 155, 158, 160, 169
Allen, 49
Allerton Gledhow, 8
Allison, Joseph, 159
Armitage, John, 10, 170
Astbury ware, 22–24, 28, 158
Atkinson, Robert, 168

BARKER, Samuel, 157
Barlaston, 30
Barwick, John, 16, 18, 43, 163, 165–6, 171
Batavian ware, 47
bat printing, 44
Bewick, Thomas, 54
Bingley, Thomas, 20, 155–6
black earthenware, 22, 46, 147, 149, 161, 163
black stoneware, 46–47, 55, 151, 156–7, 159, 160–1, 163
Booth, Miss, 18, 165
Boston in Kerseymere, 18
Boynton collection, 4, 40, 156, 160
Bradford, 165
Brameld & Co, 156
Brameld, George, 156
Brameld, John, 156
Brameld, Thomas, 156
Brameld, William, 156
Brandling, Charles, 5–9, 11, 13–14, 170
Brighton, 30
British Museum, x, 1
Britton, Alfred, 21
Britton, Broadbent, 21
Britton, Richard, 7, 13, 21, 143, 171–2
Britton, Warburton &, 3
Butler, Edward, 155

'C' MARK, 1
Calder, River, 155, 158
Cambridge, Fitzwilliam Museum, x, 159
Calverly, John, 33
Calvert, 166
Cartledge, Thomas, 160
Casson Close, 5, 9, 11, 13, 17, 170
Castleford Pottery, 36, 46, 51, 56, 160, 162, 164
Castle Museum, Norwich, x
cauliflower ware, 29, 30
Champion, Richard, 33
Chappel, Stephen, 3, 13, 21, 163
Chinese seal-mark, 25
clay, 3, 12, 15, 16, 26, 33, 163, 169
Clayton, Nathaniel, 19, 171
Cockpit Hill Pottery, Derby, 27, 37, 147
colour-glazed ware, 28
Cornish stone and clay, 16, 33
Cornwall, 3, 163
Cox, George, 49
Craven, Thomas, 19, 167

DAWSON, Edmund, 171
de la Bèche, Sir Henry, 1–3, 9, 14, 20, 161, 173
delftware, 22
Delhom, Miss M, 22
Denby, Mrs, 53
Dennison, Joseph, 14, 160, 165
Derby, Cockpit Hill Pottery, 27, 37, 147
Devonshire Clay, 169
dip decoration, 47
Dixon, Jeremiah, 7, 8, 11, 170–1
Don Pottery, 18, 56, 156–7, 163, 167
Don, River, 14, 155
Dorset, 3, 26, 163
Dowbrigg Closes, 7, 9, 11, 13, 172
Drawing books, 24, 26, 30, 34, 36, 41, 43, 46–48, 49–55, 58, 142, 154
D. Rhodes & Co, 31, 36, 37, 158, 164
Ducatus Leodiensis, 12
Dutch enamelling, 38, 143

ENAMELLING, 30, 36, 53–54, 158, 160, 164, 169
encrusted ware, 47
engine turning, 51, 55

FARNLEY, 162
Fenton, Miss, 54
Ferrybridge Pottery, 160
figures, 30, 35, 44
Fitzwilliam Museum Cambridge, x, 159
flint mill, 11, 13, 15, 172
Flint Mills, Thorpe Arch, 14, 15, 164
flints, 15, 163–4

'G', MARK, 1, 2
glazes, 26–27, 40
Grabham, Oxley, 160, 173
Greatbatch, William, 39, 147, 151, 154
Green, Don Pottery, 157
Green, Ebenezer, 17, 18, 20, 156, 167–8, 171
Green, George, 158
Green, John, 9, 11, 14–18, 155–6, 163–7, 171
Green, John (junior), 18, 156–7, 163
Green, Joshua, 9, 10, 11, 14–18, 155, 164–6, 171
Green, Miss Saville, 168
Green, Mrs Saville, 165
Green, Mrs (William?), 166
Green, Saville, 16, 18, 165–8, 171
Green, William, 9, 10, 14, 17, 18, 170
green-glazed ware, 29, 156
Greens, Bingley & Co, 156
Greens, Clark & Co, 157
Greens, Hartley & Co, 155

HANSON, George, 19, 20, 156, 171
Harrogate Museum, 143
Hartley, Greens & Co, 3, 18, 19, 35, 41, 55–56, 142–3, 163–4
Hartley, Mrs William, 166
Hartley, Greens & Co, 3, 18, 19, 35, 41, 55–56, 165–7, 171
Hayes, Mrs, 18, 167
Hentig, A. W., 54
Holbeck, 165
Holbeck Moor, 14, 159
Holbeck Moor Pottery, 14, 146, 160, 165
Hull, 55, 142
Humber, River, 155
Humble, Green & Co, 3, 15, 163–5
Humble, Hartley, Greens & Co, 15, 17, 155, 165–6, 168
Humble, John, 17, 171
Humble, Joseph, 17, 171
Humble, Richard, 5, 8, 11, 14, 16, 17, 165, 170–1

Humble, Thomas, 17, 171
Hunslet, 7, 12–15, 17, 18, 159, 165, 168, 170–1
Hunslet Hall Pottery, 10, 13, 159
Hunslet Moor, 7, 160, 172
Hurst, Arthur, 4, 40, 48, 156, 160, 173
Hutchins, 15
Hutchinson and Evers, 15

INGLE, John, 170

JACKFIELD, 22, 46
Jack Lane, 12, 13
Jackson, M., 54
Jewitt, Llewellyn, 4, 5, 19, 155–6, 173
John, Reuben, 160
Jubb, 18, 163

KEILLER Collection, 28
Kent, 26
Kiddell, A. J. B., 19, 169
Kidson, Joseph and Frank, 4, 5, 14, 21, 26, 30, 40, 45–46, 49, 156, 159, 160, 173
Kilnhurst, 155, 157
Knottingly, 162, 164

LANE Delft, 39
Leathley Lane Pottery, 160
Leeds Art Pottery Company, 160
Leed City Art Galleries, x, 4, 30, 38, 41, 45–46, 49, 51, 143
Leeds City Museum, x
Leeds Drawing Books, 24, 26, 30, 34, 36, 41, 43, 46–48, 49–55, 58, 142, 154
Leeds Intelligencer, 10, 16, 30, 164–8
Leeds Mercury, 19, 156, 158, 164–9
Leeds Order Books, 37, 55, 142, 156
Leeds Pattern Book, 1, 21, 25–26, 34, 41, 43, 46, 49, 56–141, 142, 149, 156, 161–2
Leeds Pottery bankruptcy, 17, 20, 167
Leeds Pottery Company, 21
Leeds Pottery flint mill, 11, 13, 15, 172
Leeds Union Pottery, 160
Liverpool, 43, 147
London Gazette, 167–8
lustre, 47–48

MALPASS, William, 155
Marryat, Joseph, 1
Marsden's Pottery. 45, 159
Maude, W. M., 14, 164
Meadow Lane Pottery, 159
Melbourne Pottery, 27, 149

Mexborough, 157
Middleton, 5, 8, 14, 15, 17, 170
Middleton Colliery, 8, 11, 13, 14, 17
Middleton Colliery Railway, 6
Mills, John, 159
Moscha ware, 54
Museum of Practical Geology, 1, 161

NEALE & Co, 36, 51
Nelson, Lord, 48
Newcastle upon Tyne, 19
Newhill Pottery, 159
New Pottery, 159
Newton, 157
North, John, 160
North Midland Railway Company, 7, 9, 170, 172
Norwich, Castle Museum, x
Nottingham, 155

PARTONS, Rev. Edward, 17, 166
Pattern Book, Leeds, 1, 21, 25–26, 34, 41, 43, 46, 49, 56–141, 142, 149, 156, 161–2
Pattern Book, Don Pottery, 157
Pattern Book, Swinton Pottery, 156
Pattern Book, Castleford, 160
pearlware, 35, 40, 42–45
pepper ware, 47
Petty & Co, 159
Petty & Rainforth, 9, 13, 14, 159
Petty, Samuel, 10, 22, 163
Pit, Miss, 24
Platt, John, 19, 32, 158, 166
Poole clay, 3, 15, 26, 163
Portobello, Battle of, 23
Pottery fields, 6, 14
Prince William V of Orange, 38
'Prodigal Son', 39, 151, 154
Public Record Office, 168

QUEEN's Blue, 54
Queen's Ware, 33, 56

RAINFORTH, 9, 163
Rainforth & Co., 159
Rawmarsh, 158
red earthenware, 22, 23, 28, 154, 169
red stoneware, 22, 24, 25, 28, 55, 146, 147, 149, 151, 154
Rhodes, David, 29, 30, 31, 36, 37, 158, 164
Rhodes, J., 21
Richard Britton & Sons, 21

Robinson and Rhodes, 29, 30, 31, 36, 37, 158, 164
Robinson, Jasper, 30, 31, 37, 164
Rockingham China Works, 20, 156
Rotherham, 19, 23, 29, 169, 170
Rothwell, 14, 170
Rothwell, Pottery, 23, 29, 32, 35, 146, 158, 168
Routh, 21
Ruperti, 19, 164
Rushey Pasture, 7–12, 17, 170–2
Russell, William, 159

SADLER and Green, 39
saltglaze, 22, 23, 27, 28, 30, 147, 149, 154, 158, 170
Samuel Wainwright & Co, 20
Schreiber, Lady Charlotte, 4, 5
Schreiber collection, 4
Scott, James, 167
Sedgfield, William, 170
Selby, 15
Shaw, Samuel, 23, 158, 169
shining black ware, 47
slip decoration, 28
Smith, John, 14, 32, 35, 45, 146, 158, 168–9
Sowter & Bromley, 157
Stirk, Benjamin, 170
Stourbridge, 162
Sussex, 15, 26
Swansea, 42, 43
Swillington Bridge Pottery, 160
Swinton Pottery, 14, 18, 20, 23, 29, 46, 47, 55, 56, 142, 155–8
Sykes, Thomas, 165

TADCASTER, 14, 164
Taunton Museum, 25
Taylor's Pottery, 159, 160
'tea-party', 39
Templehurst, 158
'The Leeds Pottery Company', 21
Thoresby, Ralph, 12
Thorpe Arch, 14, 164, 168
tinselling, 48
tortoiseshell ware, 29, 35, 36, 156, 170
Towner, Donald, 173
transfer-printing, 38, 39, 43, 143, 147
Turner, Alexander, 171
Turner & Hawley, 158
Turner, John, 147
Twigg, Joseph, 157–8

underglaze-painting, 29, 36 ,38, 39, 43, 46, 54

VICTORIA and Albert Museum, x, 1, 39, 41, 49, 53, 54, 57, 58, 142, 159, 161
Victoria Pottery, 159

WAINWRIGHT and Co., 18
Wainwright, Jane, 18
Wainwright, Samuel, 7, 9, 16, 18, 20, 21, 39, 143, 160, 163, 165–6, 171
Wakefield, 168
Wakefield Museum, 47
Wakefield, West Riding Registry of Deeds, x, 7, 8, 10, 170
Warburton & Britton, 3, 21, 163
Warburton, Joseph, 160
Warburton, William, 2, 3, 5, 9, 10, 11, 14, 162–3, 171
Watkinson, George, 170
Waugh, Bartle, 170
Wedgwood, Josiah, 16, 25, 27, 29, 30–33, 36, 39, 40, 42, 46, 51, 54, 56–57, 143, 147, 149, 151, 161, 164

West Riding Registry of Deeds, Wakefield, x, 7, 8, 10, 170
Wesley, John, 38
Wharfe, River, 14
Whieldon, Thomas, 22, 28, 29
Willett collection, Brighton, 30
William V, Prince of Orange, 38
Windmill Close, 7, 9, 11–13, 15, 17, 172
Wildblood, William and Thomas, 160
Wilson, Thomas, 1, 2, 5, 9, 14, 20, 161–2
Wood, Ralph, 44–45
Woodlesford, 160
Wortley, 12, 26, 162
Wrigglesworth, William, 171
Wright, Matthew, 19, 34, 167

yellow ware, 48, 169
Yorkshire Museum, x, 4, 39, 43, 45, 48, 159
Young, Arthur, 29, 170

The Plates

1. *Red-earthenware mug with cream-coloured terminals.
Height 3¾ in. About 1760.   Miss M. Delhom. Page 22.*

2. *Red-stoneware punch-kettle and brazier. Mark (Fig. 6: 28) impressed.*
Height of kettle 9 in. Height of brazier 5¼ in. About 1770.
Victoria and Albert Museum. Page 24.

3. *Saltglaze jug, painted in enamel colours.*
Inscribed 'Success to Mr John Calverly of Leeds.' Height 7 ins. 1773.
British Museum. Page 23.

4a. *Saltglaze teapot, painted in blue, green, yellow, pink and black.*
Buildings on the reverse. Height 4¼ in. Cf. Pl. 26a, ii.
4b. *Saltglaze teapot, enamelled as Plate 4a. Inscribed 'Miss Pit'*
Buildings on the reverse. Height 4¼ in. About 1770.
Mr and Mrs Victor Gollancz. Page 24.

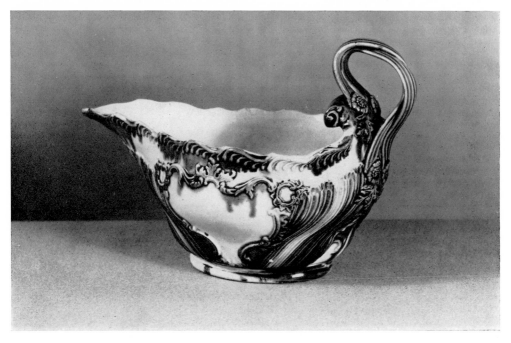

5a. *Saltglaze sauceboat. Length 7 in. Height 2¾ in. About 1770.*
Terminals, Fig. 10: 17 and Pl. 32a. Mrs R. Sargeant. Page 23.
5b. *Sauceboat, glazed in green, yellow, crimson and indigo.*
Length 7¾ in. About 1770. Terminals Fig. 10: 1.
Victoria and Albert Museum. Page 29.

6a. *Creamware teapot, decorated with a green glaze. Height 6 in. About* 1770.
Castle Museum, Norwich. Page 29.
6b. *Creamware teapot, decorated with a green glaze. Height* 5¼ *in. About* 1770.
Leeds City Art Galleries. Page 29.

7. *Creamware coffee-pot, mottled with brown manganese.*
Height 9⅞ in. About 1775. Knob, Fig. 9: 5. Terminals, Fig. 10: 11.
Leeds City Art Galleries. Page 36.

8a, i. *Creamware teapot, with applied stamped decoration coloured over in dark brown slip.*
Height 3¾ in. About 1755.
ii. *Creamware teapot, with applied stamped decoration coloured over in light brown slip.*
Height 3½ in. About 1755. Compare spout with Plate 22B, ii.
Castle Museum, Norwich. Page 28.
8b, i. *Creamware cream-jug, decorated in underglaze brownish-crimson and green.*
Height 4 in. About 1765.
ii. *Creamware teapot decorated in crimson-brown, green and yellow underglaze colours.*
Height 4½ in. About 1765. Leeds City Art Galleries. Page 29.

9a, i. *Teapot decorated in crimson-brown, green, blue and yellow underglaze colours.*
About 1770. Height 5½ in.
ii. *Teapot decorated in underglaze green. Knob Fig. 9: 4.*
About 1780. Height 5½ in.
Castle Museum, Norwich. Page 29.
9b, i. *Creamware teapot decorated in pinkish-brown underglaze colour.*
Height 3¼ in. About 1770.
ii. *Coffee-pot decorated in violet-grey underglaze colour. Height 4½ in. About 1775.*
Victoria and Albert Museum. Page 36.

10a. *Teapot decorated in violet-grey, green and golden yellow underglaze colours. Height 5¼ in. About 1780. A. F. Allbrook. Page 36.*
10b. *Punch-pot decorated in crimson-brown and green on a yellow glazed background. Height 8½ in. About 1765. Donald Towner. Page 29.*

11. *Figure group decorated in brown and green underglaze colours.*
Height 7½ in. About 1775.
Victoria and Albert Museum. Page 30.

12a. *'Sea Shell' pickle-dish (Pattern Book No. 12). Deep cream, uncoloured.*
Mark (Fig. 5: 1). Length 8 in. About 1765.
Donald Towner. Page 26.
12b. *Box with screw-top. Deep cream, uncoloured.*
Mark (Fig. 6: 26). Diam. $3\frac{1}{4}$ in. 1769.
Reproduced by permission of the syndics of the
Fitzwilliam Museum, Cambridge. Page 27.

13a, i. *Sauce-boat, deep cream, uncoloured. Length 6½ in. Height 3¼ in. About* 1770.
ii. *Teapot, deep cream, uncoloured. Height 4 in. About* 1770.
Donald Towner. Page 149.
13b, i. *Tankard, deep cream, uncoloured. Height 6 in. About* 1770.
ii. *Punch-pot, deep cream, uncoloured. Height 8½ in. About* 1770.
Donald Towner. Page 151.

14. *Jug, deep cream, enamelled in black and red.*
Height 7¼ in. Inscribed 'Thomas Store 1769'.
Victoria and Albert Museum. Page 8.

15. *Jug, deep cream, enamelled in black, with a sportsman and his dog in a landscape.*
Terminals as Plate 1. (Fig. 10: 13.) Height 7½ in. About 1770.
Donald Towner. Page 23.

16a, i. *Teapot, deep cream, enamelled by Rhodes in black and red.*
The reverse is shown on colour plate facing page 4. Height 6 in. About 1765.
ii. *Teapot, deep cream, enamelled by Rhodes in black and red.*
Houses in a landscape on the reverse. Height 5½ in. About 1765.
Donald Towner. Page 31.
16b, i. *Teapot, deep cream, enamelled by Rhodes in black and red, with touches of blue*
green and yellow on the knob and terminals. Shown on Colour plate facing page 22.
Spout, Fig. 8: 2; Knob, Fig. 9: 3; Handle, Fig. 7: 5. Height 5 in. About 1765.
ii. *Teapot, deep cream, enamelled by Rhodes in black and red, with touches of blue,*
green and yellow on the knob and terminals. Buildings on the reverse.
Knob, Fig. 9: 6. Height 5 in. About 1765.
Donald Towner. Page 31.

17a, i. *Teapot, deep cream, enamelled by Rhodes in black and red. Spout, Fig. 8: 3;
Handle, Fig. 7: 4; Knob, Fig. 9: 4, 4b. Height 5 in. About 1765.*
   ii. *Teapot, deep cream, enamelled by Rhodes in black, red, blue, rose, green and
yellow, and partly gilded. Handle, Fig. 7: 4; Spout, Fig. 8: 3. Height 5 in. About 1770.
Donald Towner. Page 31.*
17b, i. *Mug, deep cream, enamelled by Rhodes with masonic arms and symbols in
black and red. Terminals enamelled in pink, green and yellow. Height 5 in. About 1765.*
   ii. *Tankard, deep cream, enamelled by Rhodes in black and red with touches of
green on the terminals. Height 6½ in. About 1765. Donald Towner. Pages 31, 32.*

18a. *Teapot, deep cream, painted with thick green enamel. Height 4½ in. About 1770.*
Winifred Williams. Page 32.
18b. *Plate, deep cream, painted with thick green enamel. Diam. 8¾ in.*
Victoria and Albert Museum. Page 32.

19. *Coffee-pot, deep cream, enamelled in black and red, with touches of green on the terminals (Fig. 10: 2). Height 9¾ in. About 1765.*
Donald Towner. Page 31.

20a. *Chestnut basket and stand. Pale cream mark (Fig.* 5: 16).
The stand marked (Fig. 5: 2). *Height of basket* 10½ *in. Diam. of stand* 12 *in. About* 1805.
Leeds City Art Galleries. Page 34.
20b, i. *Plate, pale cream. Mark (Fig.* 5: 4). *Pattern Book No.* 42. *Diam.* 8 *in. About* 1785.
ii. *Triangular Royal Compotier, pale cream.*
Mark Fig. 5: 2 *and numeral* '3'. *Pattern Book No.* 38. *Length* 9 *in. About* 1780.
iii. *Plate, pale cream. Mark Fig.* 5: 3. *Pattern Book No.* 44. *Diam.* 9 *in. About* 1785.
Donald Towner. Page 57.

21a. *Cruet containing five castors, pale cream, inscriptions enamelled black within a red cartouche. Height 8½ in. About 1780. Leeds City Art Galleries. Page 34.*

21b, i. *Candlestick, pale cream. Height 10¾ in. About 1785.*

ii. *Candlestick, pale cream. Pattern Book No. 113. Height 11¼ in. About 1785.*

iii. *Candlestick, pale cream. Pattern Book No. 108. Height 10 in. About 1785.*

Leeds City Art Galleries. Page 57.

22a. *Ewer and Basin, pale cream. Height 10¾ in. About 1785.*
22b, i. *Two-handled sauceboat attached to stand, pale cream. Pattern Book No. 170.*
Mark Fig. 5: 6. Length 7 in. About 1785.
ii. *Coffee-pot, pale cream. Spout as Pl. 8a, ii. Terminals Fig. 10: 1. Height 7 in.*
About 1775. Donald Towner. Page 28, 58.

23. *Vase candlestick, pale cream, Pattern Book No. 116. Incised mark Fig.* 6:30. *Height* 12½ *in. About* 1785. *Victoria and Albert Museum. Pages* 35, 49, 57.

24. Cockle-pot, pale cream. Pattern Book No. 139.
Mark (Fig. 5: 10). Height 19 in. About 1780.
Donald Towner. Pages 35, 57.

25. *Centre-piece (Grand Platt Menage) with four castors and hanging baskets.*
Pale cream. Height 24 in. About 1780.
Donald Towner. Page 34.

26a, i. *Teapot, pale cream enamelled in red, yellow, green and rosy-purple.*
Handle, Fig. 7: 7; Spout, Fig. 8: 6; Knob, Fig. 9: 4, 4b. Height 4¾ in. About 1775.
ii. *Teapot, pale cream enamelled in red monochrome. Buildings on the reverse.*
Handle and terminals, Fig. 7: 7; Spout, Fig. 8: 5; Knob, Fig. 9: 4, 4b. Height 4½ in.
About 1775. Compare Plate 4a. Donald Towner. Page 37.
26b, i. *Teapot, pale cream enamelled in rosy purple, red, green, yellow and black;*
traces of gilding. Terminals, Fig. 10: 16; Spout, Fig. 8: 7;
Knob, Fig. 9: 4b with Fig. 10: 16. Height 4¾ in. About 1775.
ii. *Teapot, pale cream enamelled in dull purple, knob and terminals in deep green;*
traces of gilding. Terminals, Fig. 10: 16; Spout, Fig. 8: 7;
Knob, Fig. 9: 1. Height 4¾ in. About 1775. Donald Towner. Page 37.

27a, i. *Cup and saucer, pale cream, painted in underglaze-blue. Height of cup* 1¾ *in.,
Diam. of cup* 3 *in., Diam. of saucer* 4¾ *in. About* 1780.
ii. *Teapot, pale cream, painted in underglaze-blue. Handle and terminals,
Fig.* 7: 7; *Knob, Fig.* 9: 4, 4b. *Height* 5 *in. About* 1780. *Donald Towner. Page* 38.
27b, i. *Sugar-cup, pale cream, enamelled in crimson; terminals green.
Knob, Fig.* 9: 4, 4a. *Height* 3¼ *in. About* 1775.
ii. *Teapot, pale cream enamelled in crimson monochrome. Spout, Fig.* 8: 6;
Terminals as Plates 1, 15, *and colour plate facing page* 38, *Fig.* 10: 13; *Knob,* 9: 4, 4a.
Height 5 *in. About* 1775. *Donald Towner. Page* 37.

28a. 'Melon Terrine', pale cream, enamelled in purple, crimson, yellow and green.
Pattern Book No. 68. Height 5 in. About 1780. Leeds City Art Galleries. Page 57.
28b. Loving-cup, pale cream, enamelled in red, yellow and green. Height 7 in.
Diam. 8 in. About 1780. Donald Towner. Page 38.

29. *Coffee-pot, pale cream, enamelled in red, black, yellow, blue and green against a*
background of sponged purple (similar to Plate 32a).
Knob. Fig. 9: 46 with knob terminal Fig. 9: 1a. Height 10 in. About 1775.
Leeds City Art Galleries. Page 37.

30a, i, ii. *Coffee-pots, pale cream, enamelled in crimson, with green terminals in the same style as 30a, iii. 'HM' impressed under the cover of each. Heights, $5\frac{1}{2}$ in. and $10\frac{1}{4}$ in. Although probably Leeds, the mark may indicate the Holbeck Moor Pottery, less than $\frac{1}{2}$ mile distant from Leeds. About 1780. iii. Milk-jug, pale cream, enamelled in crimson with green terminals in the same style as 30a, i, ii. Handle and terminals, Fig. 7: 7. About 1780. Leeds City Art Galleries. Page 160.*
30b, i. *Teapot, deep cream, enamelled in black, yellow, red, green and purple; traces of gilding. The reverse as Pl. 30b, ii. Handle, Fig. 7: 3; Knob, Fig. 9: 1. Height $5\frac{1}{4}$ in. About 1775. ii. Teapot, pale cream, enamelled in black, yellow, red, green and purple. The reverse as Pl. 30b, i. Handle, Fig. 7: 3; Knob, Fig. 9: 1. Height $5\frac{3}{4}$ in. About 1775. Donald Towner. Page 37.*

31a, i. *Snuff-box, Pearlware enamelled in red, blue, yellow, green, purple and flesh.*
Height 3¾ in. About 1790. ii. Shoe-buckle, pale cream, enamelled in red, blue and green.
Incised mark 'RT'. Length 3 in. Probably Leeds. About 1785. iii. Mustard-pot, pale cream,
enamelled in red and green. Knob, Fig. 9: 4, 4b. Height 3¼ in. About 1785. iv. Box with
screw top, pale cream, enamelled in red and rosy purple, Diam. 3 in. About 1780. v. Box
with screw top, cream, enamelled in red and black. Inscribed underneath 'Peter, Brein 1773'.
Diam. 3 in. vi. Box with screw top, enamelled in red, green and purple. Diam. 3 in. About 1780.
Donald Towner. Page 37.
31b, i. *Cup and saucer, pale cream, enamelled in brownish-red, green, yellow, crimson,*
purple, blue and grey; gilded edge. Height of cup 1¾ in. Diam 3 in. Diam. of saucer 5 in.
About 1785. ii. Cup and saucer, pale cream, enamelled in red, purple, yellow, green and black.
Height of cup 1⅞ in. Diam. 3 in. Diam. of saucer 5⅛ in. About 1780. iii. Cup and saucer,
pale cream, enamelled in red, blue, green, yellow and black. Height of cup 1¾ in. Diam. 3⅛ in.
Diam. of saucer 4⅝ in. About 1775. Donald Towner. Page 37.

*32a. Teapot, pale cream, enamelled in red and green against sponged purple
in the same manner as Plate 29. Spout Fig. 8: 8; Terminals, Fig. 10: 17;
Knob, Fig. 9: 4, 4b. The terminals are identical with those on
Pl. 5a. Height 5 in. About 1775.
Reproduced by permission of the syndics of the Fitzwilliam Museum, Cambridge. Pages 23, 37.
32b. Teapot, pale cream, enamelled in Holland with 'Our Lady of Kevelaar' in red,
green, black and yellow. Impressed mark Fig. 5: 8.
Knob, Fig. 9: 4b. Terminals, Fig. 10: 11. Height 4¾ in. About 1780.
Leeds City Art Galleries. Page 38.*

33a. *Teapot, pale cream, enamelled in Holland with 'Elijah and the ravens' in black and flesh. Knob, Fig. 9:4, 4a. Handle and terminals, Fig. 7:7. Height 4¼ in. About 1780.*
Donald Towner. Page 38.
33b. *Plate, pale cream, enamelled in red, brown, green, yellow, blue and black, in Holland with portraits of the prince and princess William V of Orange on the occasion of their return from exile in 1787.*
Inscribed in black with loyal acclamations in verse. Diam. 9½ in.
Donald Towner. Page 38.

34a. *Teapot, pale cream, transfer-printed in black with 'Hagar and Ishmael' on one side; 'Abraham sacrificing Isaac' on the reverse. 'Leeds Pottery' inscribed in the print (Fig. 6: 22). Height 5¼ in. About 1780. Donald Towner. Page 38.*

34b, i. *Teapot, pale cream, transfer-printed in red with a rose spray on one side and the 'Dancing lesson' on the reverse. Flower knob, Fig. 9: 1a; Terminals, Fig. 10: 4. Height 5½ in. About 1780.*

ii. *Milk-jug, pale cream, transfer-printed in black with a spray of roses; the design enamelled over in rich green. Terminals, Fig. 10: 4. Height 5¼ in. About 1780. Donald Towner. Page 39.*

35a. *Plate, pale cream, transfer-printed in red with an allegorical scene.*
LP impressed (Fig. 5: 20). Diam. 9¾ in. About 1780.
Leeds City Art Galleries. Page 39.
35b. *Plate, pale cream, transfer-printed in red with an abbey.*
'Leeds Pottery' inscribed in the print (Fig. 6: 22a). Diam. 9⅞ in. About 1780.
Donald Towner. Page 39.

36a, b. *Two sides of the same teapot, pale cream, transfer-printed in black with 'John Wesley', and 'Love and Obedience'. 'Leeds Pottery' inscribed on both prints (Fig. 6: 23). Height 5¼ in. About 1780. Leeds City Art Galleries. Page 38.*

37a. *Teapot, pale cream, transfer-printed in black with the 'Fortune-teller' on one side and the 'Twelve Houses of Heaven' on the reverse (English Cream-coloured Earthenware, Plate 66b), the prints enamelled over in red, green, yellow, and rosy purple. Height 5¼ in. About 1780. Leeds City Art Galleries. Page 40.*

37b, i. *Mug, pale cream, transfer-printed in red with the arms of the 'Society of Bucks'. Handle, Fig. 7: 3. Height 5 in. About 1780.*

ii. *Teapot, pale cream, transfer-printed in red with the 'Tea-party' on one side the 'Shepherd' on the reverse. Height 5¼ in. About 1780. Leeds City Art Galleries. Page 39.*

38. *Figure of a flute-player, pale cream.*
Incised mark 'John Smith, 1797' (Fig. 6: 31). Height 9¾ in.
Yorkshire Museum, York. Page 45.

39a, i. *Figure of a boy with a dog. Pearlware. Mark Fig.* 5: 7. *Height* 6¼ *in.*
ii. *Figure of a falconer. Pearlware. Mark Fig.* 5: 7. *Height* 7½ *in.*
About 1790. *Leeds City Art Galleries. Page* 44.
39b, i. *Figure representing 'Spring'. Pearlware. Enamelled in bluish-green, red and black.*
Mark (Fig. 5: 7). *Height* 6¼ *in.*
ii. *Figure representing 'Winter'. Pearlware. Enamelled in red, black and bluish-green.*
Mark (Fig. 5: 7). *Height* 6¼ *in.*
iii. *Figure representing 'Summer'. Pearlware. Enamelled in bluish-green and ochre.*
Mark (Fig. 5: 7). *Height* 6¼ *in. About* 1790.
Leeds City Art Galleries. Page 44.

40. *Figure of Venus. Pearlware. Enamelled in bluish-green and red. Mark (Fig. 5: 7). Height 7¾ in. About 1790. Leeds City Art Galleries. Page 44.*

41. *Figure of Sir Isaac Newton. Pearlware. Enamelled in maroon, bluish-green, red, white and yellow. Mark (Fig. 5: 7). Height 10¼ in. About 1790. Leeds City Art Galleries. Page 44.*

42a, i, ii. *A pair of Musicians. Pearlware. Both impressed with mark (Fig. 5: 7).*
Height 7½ in. (i) Enamelled in red, yellow and black, (ii) enamelled in red, bluish-green,
yellow and black. About 1790. Leeds City Art Galleries. Page 44.
42b, i. *Bust emblematic of 'Water'. Pearlware. Enamelled in sea-green; brownish-red*
lines with traces of gilding on the pedestal. Mark (Fig. 5: 7). Height 6½ in.
ii. *Bust emblematic of 'Air'. Pearlware. Enamelled in brownish-red, with traces of*
gilding on the pedestal. Mark (Fig. 5: 7). Height 6½ in. About 1790.
Victoria and Albert Museum. Page 44.

43a. *Figure of a horse, pale cream, enamelled in light brown.*
Height of horse 15¼ in. Height of stand ¾ in. About 1790.
Leeds City Art Galleries. Page 45.
43b. *Figure of a horse. Pearlware, enamelled in black and pale blue.*
The muzzle in purplish manganese underglaze colour.
Height of horse 14¾ in. Height of Stand 1¾ in. About 1795.
Leeds City Art Galleries. Page 45.

44a. *Jug. Pearlware. Enamelled in brownish yellow, blue, and black and inscribed*
'General Mercer & Captain Moores. 1801', also 'James Gant' on the back.
Mark (Fig. 5: 2). Height 7½ in. ii. Puzzle-jug. Pearlware. Enamelled in red, pink,
orange and tints of blue. Marks (Fig. 5: 2), (Fig. 6: 25). Height 7¼ in. 1801.
Leeds City Art Galleries. Page 42.
44b, i. *Tea-caddy. Pearlware. Enamelled in various colours. Mark (Fig. 5: 13). Height 6 in.*
ii. *Plate. Pearlware. Enamelled in blue, green, purple and brown. Mark (Fig. 5: 17). Diam. 9 in.*
iii. *Jug. Pearlware. Enamelled in red and blue with gilding. Terminals, Fig. 10:11. Height 5¼ in.*
About 1790. Donald Towner. Page 42.

45a, i. *Cream jug. Black stoneware. Engine turned. Mark (Fig. 5: 18). Length 5¼ in.*
ii. *Coffee-pot. Black stoneware. Engine turned. 'Widow' knob. Mark (Fig. 5: 2). Height 10 in.*
iii. *Sugar-basin. Black stoneware. Moulded with designs in relief.*
Mark (Fig. 5: 2). Height 5 in. About 1810. Leeds City Art Galleries. Page 47.
45b, i. *Teapot. Pearlware (Batavian). The body covered in dark brown dip with*
reserves containing flowers in underglaze-blue. Flower knob (Fig. 9: 4).
Terminals (Fig. 10: 11). Height 3½ in. About 1800.
ii. *Teapot. Pearlware. Decorated in light blue and black dips and some gilding.*
Acorn knob. Height 4½ in. About 1810. Leeds City Art Galleries. Page 47.

46. *Jug. Pearlware, transfer-printed in black with the 'Vicar and Moses'. On the reverse a rhyme with that title. In front the inscription 'Success to Leeds Manufactory', the Leeds-arms of the golden fleece, and the initials J.B. and S.B. (probably for John Barwick, one of the partners of the Leeds Pottery, and his wife). Enamelled over in red, crimson, yellow, blue and green and some gilding. Height 9 in. About 1805. Yorkshire Museum, York. Page 43.*

47a, i. *Teapot, very pale cream, decorated with marbled dip in brownish red and black,
the swags touched with underglaze-green. Height 4 in. About 1805.*
ii. *Cup and saucer. Pearlware. Marbled with clays of various colours.
Border in black dip and a gilded line. Diameter of saucer 4⅞ in. About 1805.*
iii. *Teapot, very pale cream, decorated in black and cinnamon dips.*
Mark (Fig. 5: 2). Height 6½ in. About 1810. Victoria and Albert Museum. Page 47.
47b, i. *Sauce-tureen, stand and ladle. Fawn coloured ware decorated with dark green
enamel and gold lustre. Mark (Fig. 5: 18). Length of stand 7½ in. About 1819.*
ii. *Mug. Silver lustre over a brown body. Mark (Fig. 5: 18). Height 4 in. About 1818.*
Leeds City Art Galleries. Page 48.

48, i. *Dish. Pearlware. Transfer-printed in underglaze blue with the 'Willow Pattern'.*
Mark (Fig. 5: 15). Length 12½ in. About 1820.
ii. *Covered dish. Pearlware. Transfer-printed in underglaze-blue with the 'Willow Pattern'.*
(Fig. 5: 4). Width 10 in. About 1815.
Donald Towner. Page 43.